Ex Libris
Wm. J. Fay

The resonances in the dialogue of Paul's Second Letter to the Corinthians are difficult to detect unless the reader has some knowledge of the social, religious and economic situation of the community to which the apostle was writing. In this lucid and clear survey, Father Murphy-O'Connor attempts to provide such background information, which he integrates skilfully into a flowing exposition of Paul's thought. St Paul's theology thus comes to life as the complex interplay of factors which prompted him to write as he did to the Corinthians is examined and explored.

NEW TESTAMENT THEOLOGY

General Editor: Professor J. D. G. Dunn,
Department of Theology, University of Durham

The theology of the Second
Letter to the Corinthians

This series provides a programmatic survey of the individual writings of the New Testament. It aims to remedy the deficiency of available published material, which has tended to concentrate on historical, textual, grammatical and literary issues at the expense of the theology, or to lose distinctive emphases of individual writings in systematized studies of 'The Theology of Paul' and the like. New Testament specialists here write at greater length than is usually possible in the introductions to commentaries or as part of other New Testament theologies, and explore the theological themes and issues of their chosen books without being tied to a commentary format, or to a thematic structure drawn from elsewhere. When complete, the series will cover all the New Testament writings, and will thus provide an attractive, and timely, range of texts around which courses can be developed.

THE THEOLOGY OF
THE SECOND LETTER
TO THE CORINTHIANS

JEROME MURPHY-O'CONNOR, OP

Ecole Biblique et Archéologique Française, Jerusalem

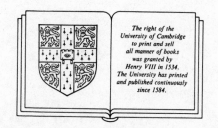

The right of the
University of Cambridge
to print and sell
all manner of books
was granted by
Henry VIII in 1534.
The University has printed
and published continuously
since 1584.

CAMBRIDGE UNIVERSITY PRESS

Cambridge
New York   Port Chester
Melbourne   Sydney

Published by the Press Syndicate of the University of Cambridge
The Pitt Building, Trumpington Street, Cambridge CB2 1RP
40 West 20th Street, New York, NY 10011, USA
10 Stamford Road, Oakleigh, Melbourne 3166, Australia

First published 1991

Printed in Great Britain at the University Press, Cambridge

British Library cataloguing in publication data
Murphy-O'Connor, Jerome
The theology of the Second Letter to the Corinthians.
1. Bible. N. T. Corinthians, 2nd. Critical studies
1. Title II. Series
227.306

Library of Congress cataloguing in publication data
Murphy-O'Connor, J. (Jerome), 1935–
The theology of the Second Letter to the Corinthians /
Jerome Murphy-O'Connor.
p.   cm. – (New Testament theology)
Includes bibliographical references and index.
ISBN 0 521 35379 3 – ISBN 0 521 35898 1 (pbk.)
1. Bible. N.T. Corinthians. 2nd – Criticism, interpretation, etc.
2. Bible. N.T. Corinthians, 2nd – Theology.
1. Title.   II. Series
BS2675.2M87   1991
227'.306–dc20   90–43043   CIP

ISBN 0 521 35379 3 hardback
ISBN 0 521 35898 1 paperback

Contents

Editor's preface

Although the New Testament is usually taught within Departments or Schools or Faculties of Theology/Divinity/Religion, theological study of the individual New Testament writings is often minimal or at best patchy. The reasons for this are not hard to discern.

For one thing, the traditional style of studying a New Testament document is by means of straight exegesis, often verse by verse. Theological concerns jostle with interesting historical, textual, grammatical and literary issues, often at the cost of the theological. Such exegesis is usually very time-consuming, so that only one or two key writings can be treated in any depth within a crowded three-year syllabus.

For another, there is a marked lack of suitable textbooks round which courses could be developed. Commentaries are likely to lose theological comment within a mass of other detail in the same way as exegetical lectures. The section on the theology of a document in the Introduction to a commentary is often very brief and may do little more than pick out elements within the writing under a sequence of headings drawn from systematic theology. Excursuses usually deal with only one or two selected topics. Likewise larger works on New Testament Theology usually treat Paul's letters as a whole and, having devoted the great bulk of their space to Jesus, Paul and John, can spare only a few pages for others.

In consequence, there is little incentive on the part of teacher or student to engage with a particular New Testament document and students have to be content with a general overview, at best complemented by in-depth study of (parts of) two or three New Testament writings. A serious corollary to this is the degree to which students are thereby incapacitated in the task of integrating their New Testament study with the rest of their Theology or Religion courses, since often they are capable only of drawing on the general overview or on a sequence of particular verses treated atomistically. The growing importance of a literary-critical approach to individual documents simply highlights the present deficiencies even more. Having been given little experience in handling individual New Testament writings as such at a theological level, most students are very ill-prepared to develop a properly integrated literary and theological response to particular texts. Ordinands too need more help than they currently receive from textbooks, so that their preaching from particular passages may be better informed theologically.

There is need therefore for a series to bridge the gap between too brief an introduction and too full a commentary where theological discussion is lost among too many other concerns. It is our aim to provide such a series. That is, a series where New Testament specialists are able to write at greater length on the theology of individual writings than is usually possible in the introductions to commentaries or as part of New Testament Theologies, and to explore the theological themes and issues of these writings without being tied to a commentary format or to a thematic structure provided from elsewhere. The volumes seek both to describe each document's theology, and to engage theologically with it, noting also its canonical context and any specific influence it may have had on the history of Christian faith and life. They are directed at those who already have one or two years of full-time New Testament and theological study behind them.

James D. G. Dunn
University of Durham

Abbreviations

AB	Anchor Bible
AnBib	Analecta Biblica
ANRW	*Aufstieg und Niedergang der romischen Welt*
AusBR	*Australian Biblical Review*
BA	*Biblical Archaeologist*
BAR	*Biblical Archaeology Review*
BGBE	Beiträge zur Geschichte der biblischen Exegese
BHT	Beiträge zur historischen Theologie
BNTC	Blacks New Testament Commentary
CBQ	*Catholic Biblical Quarterly*
EB	Etudes Bibliques
ETL	*Ephemerides Theologicae Lovanienses*
FRLANT	Forschungen zur Religion und Literatur des alten und neuen Testaments
HTR	*Harvard Theological Review*
ICC	International Critical Commentary
JBL	*Journal of Biblical Literature*
NJBC	*New Jerome Biblical Commentary*
NovTSup	Novum Testamentum, Supplements
NTS	*New Testament Studies*
RB	*Revue Biblique*
RechBib	Recherches Bibliques
SBL	Society of Biblical Literature
SBLDS	Society of Biblical Literature Dissertation Series
SBT	Studies in Biblical Theology
ScrB	*Scripture Bulletin*
SNTS	Society for New Testament Studies
TDNT	*Theological Dictionary of the New Testament*

TF	Theologische Forschung
TS	Theological Studies
WUNT	Wissenschaftliche Untersuchungen zum neuen Testament
ZNW	*Zeitschrift für die neutestamentliche Wissenschaft*

PART I

Introduction

CHAPTER I

Life in Corinth

The similarity between Paul's letters is less marked than their differences. One can sense in each the presence of the same basic theological approach, but the aspects that he highlights vary from epistle to epistle. The reason for this is that Paul never wrote just for the sake of communicating ideas. In fact, with the exception of Romans, he never wrote except when the need was forced upon him by information from one of the churches he had founded. Each letter, therefore, is a response, part of a dialogue whose agenda was established by his interlocutors, and he emphasizes what his readers needed to hear at a particular moment in their history. This dialogical element is more marked in the Corinthian correspondence than in other letters. But we only hear Paul's voice; what he says becomes really intelligible only to the extent that we can reconstruct the theological positions and social attitudes of his readers.

THE CITY OF CORINTH[1]

The Christian community at Corinth was but another touch of colour in the variegated mosaic of a great city. Its members were not foreigners but residents. They came from the city and were conditioned by its tone and temper, by its history and

[1] The textual and archaeological material on which this description is based is conveniently assembled in my *St. Paul's Corinth* (Wilmington, 1983). See also my 'The Corinth that St. Paul Saw', *BA* 47 (1984), 147–59; and V. P. Furnish, 'Corinth in Paul's Time – What Can Archaeology Tell Us?', *BAR* 15, 3 (May–June 1988), 14–27.

institutions. The problems which developed in the Corinthian community were very different from those which beset the Galatians, because their backgrounds were so diverse. Celtic tribes living on the vast prairies of central Anatolia had little in common with the inhabitants of a great commercial centre situated at a major crossroads of the ancient world.

Inside its 10 km city wall anchored by the height of Acrocorinth, Corinth sat virtually astride the 6 km-wide isthmus linking the Peloponnese to mainland Greece. This gave it control over north–south trade. It had two harbours, Lechaeum on the Corinthian Gulf and Cenchreae on the Saronic Gulf. These acted as the main channel for east–west trade because sea travel around the southern tip of the Peloponnese was so dangerous that it had given rise to the proverb 'When you double Cape Maleae forget your home' (Strabo, *Geography* 8: 6.20). The coffers of Corinth were always full, and from the time of Homer (*Iliad* 2:570) the adjective associated with Corinth was 'wealthy'.

The prime economic position of Corinth led to its refounding by Julius Caesar in 44 BC as *Colonia Laus Julia Corinthiensis*, just a century after its destruction by Rome because of its involvement in the Achaean League. Caesar gave it an administrative structure parallel to that of republican Rome. Four magistrates were elected each year who became eligible for membership of the city council after going out of office. When Achaia became a senatorial province in 27 BC it was governed by a proconsul who resided in Corinth. Appointed by the Roman Senate, each proconsul served for a year, and Paul's founding visit to Corinth is dated by his encounter with the proconsul Lucius Iunius Gallio (AD 51–2). Latin remained the official language of the city until the early second century AD, but for the majority Greek was the language of business and social life.

The new settlers were for the most part freedmen, former slaves hailing originally from Greece, Syria, Judea and Egypt. They had to start by robbing graves, but their enterprise and industry quickly led to the re-establishment of industry and trade. Once the colony was seen to be securely based, it attracted entrepreneurs from the major trading countries of the eastern Mediterranean. Such infusions of new capital in a prime commercial situation generated more wealth. Two factors attest the increasing prosperity of Corinth: the number of monumental buildings erected in the city centre during the reigns of Augustus (31 BC–AD 14) and Tiberius (AD 14–37); and the ability of the city to host once again the Isthmian Games, which were second in importance only to the Olympic Games. The vast expenditure which the Isthmian Games involved was the responsibility of the citizen elected as president, but the financial gain consequent on the presence of huge crowds of visitors benefited even small businesses. All this development demanded banking facilities, and by the early first century AD Corinth was an important financial centre.

The religious and ethnic diversity of Corinth is graphically attested by the remains of temples and shrines: the gods and goddesses of Greece are well represented; Egyptian influence is documented by the worship of Isis and Serapis; a temple near the forum witnesses to the cult of the emperor. Nothing yet discovered betrays a Jewish presence, but Philo (*Delegation to Gaius*, 281) says that there was a large and vital Jewish community at Corinth in the first century AD.

The ethos of Corinth is best illustrated by the proverb 'Not for everyone is the voyage to Corinth' (Horace, *Letters* 1:17.36; Strabo, *Geography* 8:6.20). It meant that only the strong and ruthless could survive the intense competitiveness of a wide-open boom town. Corinth had no hereditary patrician class to give it the stately dignity that an ancient university city such as Athens enjoyed. Its prominent citizens were all *nouveaux riches*. The only Corinthian tradition which the new colony respected was commercial success. It was every man for himself and the weak went to the wall.

Wealth, however, is a fragile base for self-esteem; it can vanish as quickly as it came. Contrary to what has been widely accepted, the dominant mythical figure at Corinth was not Aphrodite but Sisyphus. Described by Homer as 'the craftiest of men' (*Iliad* 6:154), he was one of the legendary kings of Corinth. On his return to Hades, after having once tricked the lord of the underworld into letting him return to earth, he was condemned ever to roll a rock to the top of a hill. As he neared the summit it would slip from his hands and he would have to begin all over again. For the Corinthians and many others his task symbolized the futility of existence. The most that could be hoped for was the temporary success of the trickster; the future was in no way secure. It was an age of anxiety.[2]

Even if Paul did not know that there was an interior void to be filled, there were a number of reasons why he chose boisterous, brawling, bustling Corinth as his first main missionary base; the second was to be Ephesus, which resembled it in many respects. Corinth was open to new ideas in a way that more traditional cities were not. If Christianity could be implanted in such a hostile environment, it would be evidence of its intrinsic power to change the world. Those from afar who came to the city on business or as visitors to the Isthmian Games might become converts who would bring the faith back to their own people. This intense traffic assured him of excellent communications. In the travelling season there were always ships going east and west as well as traders going north and south with whom he could send his messages.

THE CHURCH AT CORINTH

According to Acts 18:11, Paul's founding visit to Corinth lasted eighteen months. His encounter with the proconsul Gallio (Acts 18:12) permits us to specify that this visit ran from the spring of AD 50 to the late summer of AD 51. We are told that he worked as a tent-maker together with Aquila and Priscilla (Acts 18:1-3); and in fact they would have had plenty of business. Those taking passage on a ship had to have small tents to protect them from sun and spray on board, and to shelter them when they camped at night on a lonely beach. The Isthmian Games were celebrated in the spring of AD 51 and influenced Paul's imagery in 1 Corinthians 9:24-5. The visitors from abroad were housed in tents, and the shopkeepers of

---

[2] On this little-discussed aspect of life in antiquity see especially E. R. Dodds, *Pagan and Christian in an Age of Anxiety. Some Aspects of Religious Experience from Marcus Aurelius to Constantine* (Cambridge, 1965).

Corinth who moved out to Isthmia, to supply their needs used tents in which to display their wares. To be gainfully employed was important to Paul. At Corinth parasites got short shrift (Alciphron, *Letters of Parasites* n. 24; 3:60), and he did not want receptivity to his preaching to be conditioned by acceptance of a financial burden (1 Cor. 9:1–18).[3]

The names of a number of his converts can be gleaned from Acts 18:2–17, 1 Cor. 16:15–19, and Rom. 16:1–3, 21–3. There are sixteen names in all. Since some were converted with their households, and presumably all were married, the minimum membership of the community must have been between forty and fifty. It may have been considerably larger, because Paul certainly does not list even every male member.

Efforts have been made to determine the status of these individuals in order to get some idea of the social stratification of the Christian community at Corinth.[4] Many factors contribute to fixing status, e.g. racial origins, legal status, personal status, occupation, religion, sex, wealth, etc. Some indicators carry more weight than others, depending on the social context, and in addition are conditioned by the attitude of the person judging. Many members of the Corinthian community rate high on one or more scales but low on others. Aquila, for example, rates high in terms of wealth and gender, because he was a male and travelled considerably, but low in terms of legal status, occupation and religion, because he was a Jew who worked with his hands and was only a resident alien at Corinth. Phoebe was patroness of the church at Cenchreae, which would give her a rank equal to Gaius who hosted the whole church. But he was a man and she a woman, and that made a significant difference.

This inconsistency in the way people of apparently similar station were actually judged in status and rank led to dissatisfaction with the status quo. Individuals afflicted with status

---

[3] See, R. E. Hock, *The Social Context of Paul's Ministry. Tentmaking and Apostleship* (Philadelphia, 1980).

[4] The initial attempt by G. Theissen, *The Social Setting of Pauline Christianity. Essays on Corinth* (Philadelphia, 1982), 69–119, should be corrected in the light of W. A. Meeks, *The First Urban Christians. The Social World of the Apostle Paul* (New Haven, 1983), 51–73.

inconsistency are mobile and restless. They question and strive for change in order to resolve the ambiguities and contradictions under which they live. Certain Corinthians were attracted by the paradoxes (e.g. a crucified Saviour) with which Paul's gospel abounded, perhaps because these resonated with their perception of reality. They saw the new egalitarian community that he proposed as an alternative environment in which their energies and talents could be deployed with a freedom that society denied them. This explanation of why Paul quickly won converts at Corinth is confirmed by the absence of anyone from the very top or bottom of the Greco-Roman social scale. There were no patricians or landed aristocrats, nor were there any field or mine slaves. In other words, those who had no expectations (since they had everything) and those who had no hope (since no improvement seemed possible) were not attracted to Christianity.

Another aspect exhibited by the Corinthian community is brought to light in 1 Corinthians 1:26–8, which is as close to a social description of the membership as Paul ever gets. He contrasts a minority referred to as 'wise, powerful and wellborn' with the majority who are 'stupid, weak, base and despised'. All these terms occur regularly in classical Greek literature to express the basic class distinction between 'rich' and 'poor'. Thus, for example, Aristotle says, 'inasmuch as oligarchy is defined by birth, wealth and education, the characteristics of the mass of citizens are thought to be the opposite of these, low birth, poverty and vulgarity' (*Politics*, 6:1.9 1317b39–41). It is not to be thought that this class division was completely overcome by the idealism implicit in conversion to Christ. Paul in fact has to condemn wealthy members of the community for the way they humiliate the 'have-nots' (1 Cor. 11:21–2).

This, however, was not the only consequence. With his customary insight Aristotle points out that 'Party strife is always due to inequality' (*Politics*, 5:1.6 1301b27), and Paul bemoans the jealousy and strife which have led Corinthian Christians to form party factions (1 Cor. 1:12; 3:3–4). On the basis of a pattern common in Greek cities of the period, it would appear that certain wealthy members of the community exploited the dependence of poor believers to carve out for themselves power bases within the church.[5] This tendency was accentuated by the fact that no averagely wealthy house of the period could comfortably receive the whole community. Paul's use of the adjective 'whole' in 1 Corinthians 14:23 and Romans 16:23 suggests that such reunions were rare. The community normally met in sub-groups, a series of house churches whose relative isolation from one another encouraged divisions and differences.[6]

[5] This suggestive insight is developed by L. L. Welborn, 'On the Discord in Corinth: 1 Corinthians 1–4 and Ancient Politics', *JBL* 106 (1987), 85–111.

[6] House churches and their problems are discussed by R. Banks, *Paul's Idea of Community. The Early Housechurches in their Historical Setting* (Sydney, 1979). He has also published a fascinating imaginative reconstruction, *Going to Church in the First Century. An Eyewitness Account* (Chipping Norton, NSW, 1980).

CHAPTER 2

The background of 2 Corinthians

Although 2 Corinthians is separated by only a year from
1 Corinthians (2 Cor. 8:10; 9:2; cf. 1 Cor. 16:1–4) and is
addressed to the same community, it is a very different
document. Apart from minor outbursts, the tone of 1 Corinthians is calm and measured, and the matters discussed are
clearly delineated and organized. Such cool logic is absent in
2 Corinthians. A sense of injury pervades the letter, and the
tension under which Paul labours is perceptible in the associative links that give rise to digressions and repetitions, and make
certain transitions difficult to explain.

THE INTEGRITY OF 2 CORINTHIANS

One very radical explanation is offered for these digressions
and repetitions. Thus, for example, because 7:5ff. seems to be
the natural continuation of 2:12–13, it is argued that an editor
forced them apart in order to insert 2:14–7:4, which actually
belonged to another letter written by Paul to Corinth. When
the same type of explanation is applied to similar problems, the
result is the theory that 2 Corinthians is a combination of five
originally distinct letters.[7]

Like many commentators, I do not find that the hard
transitions in chapters 1–9 imply such a degree of discontinuity
as to demand such a radical partition theory. On the other
hand, however, it is perfectly clear that chapters 10–13 cannot
be the continuation of chapters 1–9. It is psychologically

---

[7] For example, G. Bornkamm, 'The History of the Origin of the So-Called Second
Letter to the Corinthians', *NTS* 8 (1961–2), 258–64.

impossible that Paul should suddenly switch from the celebration of reconciliation with the Corinthians (1–9) to savage reproach and sarcastic self-vindication (10–13). Such an attack on the Corinthians would have undone everything he had tried to achieve in chapters 1–9.[8]

If chapters 1–9 and 10–13 are in fact two separate letters, which came first? Some scholars date chapters 10–13 before chapters 1–9, because they claim that the severe and often brutal tone indicates that it must be identified with the Sorrowful Letter, to which Paul refers in 2:4 and 7:8.[9] Such a solution, however, is unacceptable. It is clear from 2:5–8 that the Sorrowful Letter was occasioned by the behaviour of someone who insulted Paul. Such an individual is never even alluded to in chapters 10–13, which are concerned with the damage done to the community by false apostles. The content of chapters 10–13, therefore, excludes its identification with the Sorrowful Letter, and this in turn removes the only reason for dating this letter prior to chapters 1–9.

The bitter tone of chapters 10–13 is better explained if it was written subsequently to chapters 1–9.[10] Clear hints of serious tension can be detected beneath the conciliatory tone of chapters 1–9. There had been a reconciliation of sorts between Paul and the Corinthians. Even though he was not entirely convinced that the root of the trouble had been completely eradicated, he desperately wanted to believe that the Corinthians had definitely decided for him and against his opponents within the community. It is natural to wish troubles behind one, but Paul wanted to be free to move into virgin territory and found new churches. When news came that the

---

8 Recently F. Young and D. F. Ford have tried to justify the change in emotional tone in chapters 10–13 by arguing that the genre of 2 Corinthians is that of a forensic defence whose common pattern demanded a highly charged emotional peroration which is to be found in chapters 10–13 (*Meaning and Truth in 2 Corinthians* (London, 1987), 27–59). While the first part of this hypothesis is acceptable, the second shatters on the rock of chapters 8–9. A plea for money, even for others, has no place in an *apologia*.

9 For example, A. Plummer, *A Critical and Exegetical Commentary on the Second Epistle of St Paul to the Corinthians* (ICC; Edinburgh, 1915), xxvii–xxxvi.

10 So, rightly, C. K. Barrett, *The Second Epistle to the Corinthians* (BNTC; London, 1973), 243–5; V. P. Furnish, *II Corinthians* (AB; Garden City, NY, 1984), 35–41.

situation in Corinth had deteriorated to the point where his opponents appeared to have the upper hand, he was deeply hurt and disappointed. His frustration inevitably found expression in the savage reproaches and sarcastic self-vindication of chapters 10–13.

OPPOSITION TO PAUL AT CORINTH

Letters A (chaps. 1–9) and B (chaps. 10–13) reflect a developing situation at Corinth. Opposition to Paul, which is only hinted at in Letter A, is brought out into the open in Letter B. Neither letter, therefore, can be correctly understood unless we have a clear idea of who Paul's adversaries were and what they stood for. Indeed, why he speaks in a certain way and why he develops some aspects of his theology rather than others were determined by the agenda of his opponents.

Scholarly opinion is deeply divided on the question of the identity of the opposition at Corinth and its theological stance.[11] The evidence contained in Letters A and B points in two different directions. Some clues indicate that the opponents were Judaizers of Palestinian origin, who maintained that Gentile believers were bound by the Mosaic Law.[12] Other hints, however, seem to suggest Hellenistic-Jewish wandering preachers, who were convinced that their eloquence, ecstatic experiences and miracle-working power demonstrated their possession of the Holy Spirit.[13] Thus, one group of scholars maintains that the opponents were law-observant Jewish Christians, while another insists that they were Hellenistic-Jewish propagandists.

Both of these positions tend to emphasize one set of clues at the expense of the other. Inevitably, evidence that does not fit with the conclusion adopted is either ignored or given a meaning incompatible with the natural interpretation. In recent years scholars dissatisfied with such one-sided

---

[11] An excellent survey is given by V. P. Furnish, *II Corinthians* 48–54.

[12] See, J. J. Gunther, *St. Paul's Opponents and their Background: a Study of Apocalyptic and Jewish Sectarian Teaching* (NovTSup; Leiden, 1973), 299–303.

[13] The pre-eminent representative of this view is D. Georgi, *The Opponents of Paul in Second Corinthians* (Philadelphia, 1986).

treatments of data in the letters have developed a more sophisticated understanding of the situation at Corinth, which attempts to do justice to all the evidence. In essence, they suggest that intruders from outside the community formed an alliance with disaffected members within the Corinthian church.[14] These two groups had different orientations, but they found common ground in their opposition to Paul. Their union was fragile, and in order to maintain even a semblance of unity each had to make concessions to the other, with the result that both changed somewhat in the process.

The fact that one group of opponents needed letters of recommendation (3:1) labels them as non-Corinthian Christians. Within the context in which they are presented Paul evokes the Mosaic Law (3:3) in a negative way and is forced to make a distinction in the concept of new covenant (3:6). The intruders thought of themselves as 'servants of the new covenant' because this permitted them to harmonize their belief that the eschaton had been inaugurated in Christ with their view that the Law, as in Jeremiah 31:33, enjoyed permanent validity for Christians. This was the classical position of Judaizers coming from the conservative Jerusalem church, and this identification is confirmed by Paul's appropriation of their claim to be both Israelites and Hebrews (11:22).

To identify the intruding Judaizers' allies at Corinth we have to go back to 1 Corinthians.[15] Although Paul mentions four factions (1:12), a close reading of the letter makes it progressively clearer that most of the problems at Corinth arose because of the radically divisive religious stance of one particular group within the community.

These believed that their possession of 'wisdom' made them 'perfect' (2:6). As possessors of 'the Spirit which is from God' (2:12) they were 'spirit-people' (2:15). They thought of them-

[14] This is a development of C. K. Barrett's insight that the intruders were 'Corinthianized'; 'Paul's Opponents in II Corinthians', *NTS* 17 (1970–1), 233–54, see especially 251 and 254.

[15] Young and Ford are among the very few to stress this obvious point (*Meaning and Truth*, 44–8). The majority, represented by Furnish (*II Corinthians*, 50), insist on treating 1 and 2 Corinthians as absolutely different cases, forgetting that they were separated by only one year and that the composition of the community at Corinth had not changed significantly in the interval.

selves as 'filled [with divine blessings]', 'wealthy', 'kings' (4:8), 'wise', 'strong' and 'honoured' (4:10). They looked down on others in the community as 'children' capable of imbibing only 'milk' (3:1), and considered them to be 'fools' who were 'weak' and 'dishonoured' (4:10). Such terminology reflects Philo's distinction between the heavenly and earthly man. All the key words appear in two passages of a single work, *De Sobrietate* 9–11 and 55–7, and each individual term is extensively paralleled in other works of the great Jewish philosopher from Alexandria. For convenience, I shall call this group the Spirit-people.[16]

The Spirit-people presumably imbibed their Philonism from Apollos, an Alexandrian-Jewish convert who had probably studied under Philo (Acts 18:24), and who ministered at Corinth after Paul's first visit (1 Cor. 3:6; Acts 19:1). Their intention was not to turn away from Christianity but to deepen their faith. Paul had provided only the very basic elements (1 Cor. 2:2), and they seem to have found in Apollos an orator trained to develop a synthesis, who could give their faith speculative depth by employing Philo's philosophical framework.

The desire of the Spirit-people for a genuine theology was entirely legitimate, and the means they adopted to achieve it were unexceptional. In a real sense they were the precursors of the development of speculative theology in the western church. Paul, I suspect, was unhappy in principle with their theorizing because it was time taken from the practice of charity. Thus he was not disposed to give them a fair hearing. Such latent antagonism was fuelled by the disparaging comparison which the Spirit-people drew between himself and Apollos. The latter's eloquence and impressive presence marked him out as a spiritual leader, and these were precisely the qualities which they considered Paul lacked (2 Cor. 10:10). In their eyes he did

---

[16] The existence of this group in 1 Corinthians has been demonstrated by R. A. Horsley, 'Pneumatikos versus Psychikos: Distinction of Status among the Corinthians', *HTR* 69 (1976), 269–88, and 'Wisdom of Word and Words of Wisdom in Corinth', *CBQ* 39 (1977), 224–39. For their continuing existence in 2 Corinthians, see my 'Pneumatikoi in 2 Corinthians', *Proceedings of the Irish Biblical Association* 11 (1988), 59–66.

not possess the Spirit or wisdom. It would be asking too much of human nature to expect Paul to treat such criticism with dispassionate objectivity, and 1 Corinthians amply demonstrates to what extent he was an ordinary emotional human being. He makes no real effort to enter into their thought-world, and in 1 Corinthians 2:6–3:4 he holds their intellectual pretensions up to ridicule.

The effect of 1 Corinthians in Corinth must have been to alienate the Spirit-people completely. They had been publicly humiliated when the letter was read to the assembly, and their pride sought revenge. Thus they were predisposed to welcome the Judaizing intruders, not because they were sympathetic to the message they preached, but because they knew it would disturb Paul intensely. The figure of Moses furnished a tenuous common ground. The Judaizers revered him as the Law-giver, while the Spirit-people probably saw him as the perfect wise man who embodied all the Hellenistic virtues. In order to maintain their foothold in the community, however, the Judaizers had to adapt to the Spirit-people's expectations of religious leadership, which Paul had refused to do. In consequence, they were led to stress their superior qualifications. They had to preach themselves (2 Cor. 4:5; 10:12) by advertising their visions and revelations (2 Cor. 12:1) and their miracles (2 Cor. 12:12). If they did not know them already, they would have had to adopt the conventions of Hellenistic rhetoric in order to flatter the sensibilities of their hosts. Such 'Corinthianization' of the Judaizers is the best explanation of the combination of apparently incompatible traits that appear in 2 Corinthians.

BETWEEN I CORINTHIANS AND 2 CORINTHIANS

In all probability 1 Corinthians was written from Ephesus in May, AD 54 (1 Cor. 16:8). Shortly afterwards, Timothy returned from Corinth (1 Cor. 4:17; 16:11). His report on the state of the church there forced Paul to abandon his plan to go to Macedonia (1 Cor. 16:5) and to go instead to Corinth (2 Cor. 13:2). The reception he got there was anything but warm, and he left to go to Macedonia, presumably to allow a cooling off period, because he planned to return to Corinth (2 Cor. 1:16). *En route*, he decided that another visit so soon would do more harm than good, and he returned to Ephesus, whence he wrote the Sorrowful Letter (2 Cor. 2:1–4). Such chopping and changing in his travel plans did nothing to endear him to the Corinthians. Rather, it confirmed their opinion of him as a vacillating and weak personality.

The Sorrowful Letter, which has been lost, was carried to Corinth by Titus, and Paul was desperately anxious to know what effect it had had. His relationship with the community was balanced on a knife edge. When he was forced to leave Ephesus (Acts 19:23–41) in the late summer of AD 54, Paul went north to Troas (2 Cor. 2:12), which lay on the route that he expected Titus to take on his return. Paul began a successful ministry at Troas, but his impatience quickly got the better of him, and he took ship for Macedonia, where he met Titus (2 Cor. 2:13; 7:5).

They spent the winter of AD 54–5 together in Philippi or Thessalonica. Titus brought Paul up to date on the situation at Corinth, and was able to assure him that the Sorrowful Letter had had its effect; the community deeply regretted the incident (2 Cor. 7:8–11). Paul's sense of relief establishes the basic tone of Letter A (2 Cor. 1–9), which was sent in the spring of AD 55. His warm, sensitive nature opened in generosity to the Corinthians, and he does his best to clear up any misunderstandings. Despite the protestations of repentance, however, he was shrewd enough to recognize that something had to be done about the Spirit-people. He had learnt from his terrible error of judgement in 1 Corinthians, and he changed his tactics completely. He opted for a discreet indirect approach without any overt criticism. Presumably with the aid of Apollos, who had been with him at Ephesus (1 Cor. 16:12), he makes a serious effort to enter into their thought-world and exhibits the gospel of Christ in a light designed to appeal to their religious sensitivities. At the same time, he is concerned to exhibit the message of the Judaizers in a way that would guarantee its unattractiveness to the Spirit-people. This delicate two-pronged operation is carried out with a subtlety that excites admiration for Paul's adaptability and the flexibility of his mind. It deserved to succeed.

Having spent the winter with the Macedonian churches, and with the problems of the Corinthian church behind him, Paul's spirits rose with the new sap of the spring of AD 55. After several years of maintenance work he was free again to pursue his authentic vocation as a founder of churches. In early summer he went west along the Via Egnatia into the virgin territory of Illyricum (Rom. 15:19). Sometime during the summer his ministry there was disrupted by very bad news from Corinth.

Letter A had cut the ground from under the feet of the Judaizers, who in response redoubled their attacks on Paul. They questioned his authority more radically than before. Deeply wounded and bitterly disappointed, Paul immediately reacted by lashing out angrily in Letter B (2 Cor. 10–13). He defends himself with vehemence, and in the process reveals himself to be a master of Greek rhetoric. Such a letter could only be a stop-gap, and as soon as was feasible he left Illyricum for his third visit to Corinth (2 Cor. 13:1–2), where he spent the winter of AD 55–6.

PART II

The letters

CHAPTER 3

Clearing up misunderstandings (1:1–2:13)

Two concerns dominate the opening section of 2 Corinthians. Paul has to disabuse the Corinthians of the idea that the changes in his travel plans showed him to be vacillating and basically untrustworthy. He also has to reciprocate their regret for an unfortunate incident at Corinth by showing his appreciation and forgiveness.

GREETING AND BLESSING (1:1–11)

The opening of the letter is a development of the standard superscription which is illustrated by 'Claudius Lysias to his excellency the governor Felix, greeting' (Acts 23:26). Paul qualifies himself as 'an apostle of Christ Jesus' (1:1), both in order to underline his authority, and to make it clear that his ministry had not been self-chosen. His 'sending' (apostle means 'one sent') by Christ (1 Cor. 15:8–11) was an expression of the will of God. He used this descriptive formula for the first time in 1 Corinthians 1:1 (compare 1 Thess. 1:1; 2 Thess. 1:1) because he had lost his legitimizing home base in the church at Antioch (Acts 13:1–3). After the dispute with Peter at Antioch (Gal. 2:11–14) he found that he could no longer represent a church in which the Mosaic Law was permitted to have a dominant role. This laid him open to the accusation that he had no authorization to preach, and his only defence was to insist on his commissioning by Christ. Thus, right from the beginning, we sense Paul's preoccupation with the legitimacy of his ministry, which is in fact a major theme of Letter A.

With the Corinthians to whom the letter is addressed Paul associates 'all the saints who are in the whole of Achaia' (1:1), which evokes a similar phrase in 1 Corinthians 1:2. Nothing like either appears in any other Pauline letter, and its function here is to remind the Corinthians that they were not the only church. Unlike the Galatians, they welcomed the responsibility of freedom and had no difficulty in deciding on what they thought were appropriate expressions of faith in practice. As 1 Corinthians shows, Paul could not always agree, and the suggestion here is that they should have the humility to learn from other churches (cf. 1 Cor. 11:16). Each local church, he believed, should have its own individuality, but the tradition it shares with others must be a visible reality.

With the exception of Galatians, the first paragraph in other Pauline letters is a thanksgiving motivated by the manifestations of grace in the recipients. Its replacement here by a benediction (1:3–11) appears to have been dictated by his deliverance from great danger for which he gives praise to God. Paul does not tell us what the danger was (1:8–9). The formulation does not suggest a serious illness (e.g. Gal. 4:13), and we should perhaps think of a violent episode such as the revolt of the silversmiths in Ephesus (Acts 19:23–20:1). He was convinced that death was imminent. There seemed to be no hope of getting out alive (1:9). Yet God saved him, and this was the basis of his conviction that God could and did act on behalf of those who had committed themselves to him.

From this experience Paul draws the general principle that God strengthens us in our afflictions (1:4). In the light of what follows it should not be thought that this strength is a mysterious grace. Those who have been strengthened are able to give strength to others (1:4), obviously by support, encouragement, sympathy, understanding or any of the other gestures by which we sustain others. Grace operates through human instruments. The mode that Paul highlights is example (1:6–7). The Corinthians should interpret Paul's survival of all the dangers attendant on his mission (11:22–8) as the working of God's strengthening grace. To see grace at work is itself a strengthening experience; they know that they can survive as Paul did.

It would be most unlike Paul to leave matters on a theistic level, and so it is not unexpected to find a reference to Christ (1:5). This verse is intelligible only if we recognize that Paul did not reserve the name 'Christ' for Jesus but also used it as the name of the local church: 'Your bodies are members of Christ' (1 Cor. 6:15; 12:12). Thus 'to be baptized into Christ' (Gal. 3:27; Rom. 6:3) is to participate in the rite of initiation into a Christian community. Equally 'to be in Christ' (1 Cor. 1:30; 2 Cor. 5:17) is simply to be a member of a Christian community. In Paul's mind the identity of the church with the historical Jesus is functional not mystical. As Jesus did during his lifetime, the church demonstrates the effects of grace in the world. Paul will also speak of the church as the *Body* of Christ (1 Cor. 12:12–27; Col. 1:18; 2:17) precisely in order to emphasize the physical dimension. The community does not merely talk about the power of God; the comportment of believers exhibits that power in action. In this way the church prolongs the ministry of Jesus Christ. It is Christ in action *today*. The 'sufferings of Christ', therefore, are the sufferings of the community.[17] Many of his communities suffered persecution (1 Thess. 2:14; Phil. 1:27–30) in which Paul shared by his anguish for their safety and perseverance. In such communities there were those who sustained him by their courage and dedication, which is why he can say 'so through Christ we share abundantly in strength also' (1:5).

CANCELLED VISITS AND THEIR CONSEQUENCES (1:12–2:13)

When writing 1 Corinthians, Paul planned to reach Corinth at the end of the summer of AD 54 and spend the following winter there. He explicitly states that he did not want to make just a brief visit (1 Cor. 15:5–6), yet that was in fact what he did early in the summer (2 Cor. 2:1). On that occasion he promised to

---

[17] J. Dunn thinks that it is a question of the sufferings of the last days which began with the passion of Christ (*Jesus and the Spirit. A Study of the Religious and Charismatic Experience of Jesus and the First Christians as Reflected in the New Testament* (Philadelphia, 1975), 332).

return (1:16), but he did not (1:23; 2:1), and instead wrote the Sorrowful Letter (2:4). Not unreasonably, there were those at Corinth who considered him unstable, a vacillator who eagerly said 'Yes, yes' when he thought his interlocutors expected agreement and 'No, no' when he considered they wanted a negative response (1:17).[18] What credence could be given to the gospel preached by someone so unreliable?

In reply, Paul asserts that his conscience is clear. His sense of mission controls his decisions, not the self-serving calculations of fallen humanity (1:12). Knowing the propensity of the Corinthians to misread his letters (e.g. 1 Cor. 5:9–11), he has to beg them to pay attention to what he actually says and not to impose their own interpretation on his words (1:13). The warning is also necessary for modern readers because Paul's argument for his dependability (1:18–22) is rather convoluted.

God is utterly reliable (1:18a) because he has fulfilled all his promises. Christ brought to reality in history all the various forms in which God promised salvation (1:20a). He is the seed of Abraham (Gal. 3:16), the Davidic Messiah (Rom. 1:4), the last Adam (1 Cor. 15:45), life, wisdom, righteousness and sanctification (1 Cor. 1:30). Moreover, Christ was completely dependable. He never wavered in his commitment, and his whole existence was the affirmative response that God expected, 'an enduring Yes' (1:19). It is this God, however, who commissioned Paul (1:21). The verb *chriein* means literally 'to anoint' and it is used here because of its relation to *Christos* 'the Anointed One'. To bring out this play on words the phrase should be translated: God 'christed' Paul, marking him with a seal as belonging to Christ, and gifting him with the Spirit as an earnest of future fulfilment (1:22).[19] In simpler terms, God has made Paul another Christ, which means that he grants him

---

[18] F. Young has argued that 1:17b should be rendered 'Or do I make plans at the human level so that it's in my hands that yes be yes and no be no' (F. Young and D. F. Ford, *Meaning and Truth in 2 Corinthians* (London, 1987), 101–2). While possible grammatically, this interpretation shifts the blame to God in a way which scarcely does justice to Paul's view of divine human co-operation.

[19] J. Dunn grasps the nuance perfectly in writing 'The Spirit was the presentness of future blessing' (*Jesus and the Spirit*, 311), and draws attention to the close link Paul here establishes between Jesus and the Spirit; there is no Spirit apart from Jesus (*ibid.*, 318). The importance of this will become apparent only later in the epistle.

the grace to be as totally reliable as Christ was. To drive home this point Paul notes that his preaching was entirely unambiguous whether he was speaking of God (1:18) or of Christ (1:19); there was never any wavering in his presentation. At this point Paul breaks off and leaves his readers to draw the obvious conclusion: namely, that his travels in the service of the gospel were governed by his vision of his mission and his ✓ message.

Having established that he could not be a vacillator, Paul now goes on to explain why, instead of returning to Corinth, he wrote the Sorrowful Letter. Paul never says exactly what happened during his second visit to Corinth. From slender hints in 2:5–11 and 7:8–12 it has been deduced that he was insulted by an individual and that the community did not come to his defence but remained chillingly neutral.[20] It was this latter that hurt Paul most. They were his children (1 Cor. 4:14–15) and they had not taken his side. After he had left, he became convinced that a cooling-off period would not be enough. There was a real risk that a return visit would lead to a shouting match that would only further embitter relations (2:1) or that he would be forced into an authoritarian position that was unpalatable to him (1:23–4). He wanted to be able to present his case without interruption and a letter appeared to be the best solution (1:3).

Deeply hurt as he was, Paul did not use the letter to vent his anger, which means it was a very different document from Letter B (2 Cor. 10–13), but to articulate his love for the Corinthians. His object was not to command obedience but to warm their hearts towards him. The effect of the letter is dealt with in 7:8–12. The affection of the Corinthians for Paul was rekindled and they deeply regretted the hurt they had caused. Here, however, after a rather feeble joke (2:2) designed to lighten the atmosphere, Paul is concerned with an action taken by the Corinthians as a result of their repentance.

They had punished the one who had insulted Paul, and he thinks that it should now stop lest the penalty lose its remedial

---

[20] C. K. Barrett, '*Ho Adikesas* (2 Cor. 7:12)', in *Verborum Veritas* (*Festschrift* for G. Stählin; ed. O. Bocher and K. Haacker; Wuppertal, 1970), 149–57.

value (2:6). Paul's concern for the offender here is less important than the insight we are given into his understanding of
what a local church is. He had not dictated the line the
community should take. He would use his authority to challenge by writing the Sorrowful Letter, but he would not impose
a solution. They had to work out the will of God for themselves
(cf. Col. 1:9–10); only thus could they accept and exercise
responsibility. They had to discover the authentic expression
of love and formulate their own vision of truth. If they made
mistakes Paul would correct them and leave them to start their
quest anew. Thus he ensured that autonomy would not lead to
anarchy.

Because of the centrality of community in his thought Paul
also saw every sin as having a social dimension; the sin of one
had an effect on all (2:5; cf. 1 Cor. 5:6–7). The basis for this
view was his understanding of the basis of human freedom.
The force of good example within the community, which
provided support, encouragement and inspiration, held at bay
the pressures of the false value-system of the world, thus giving
the members the opportunity to develop authentically in
freedom. The selfishness of one (sin is fundamentally selfish)
diminished the protection that the members afforded one
another, and thereby put others at risk. Any diminution of the
love that the members owed one another created a debt
('Forgive us our debts as we have forgiven our debtors' (Matt.
6:12), which impoverished all.

This idealistic vision did not blind Paul to the realities of
community life, and he warns the Galatians 'You have been set
free for freedom' (5:1) – the point being that they have to give
reality to their freedom, which is not a possession of the
individual but a property of the community. If the triumph of
'the desires of the spirit' (authentic values) over the 'desires of
the flesh' (false values; Gal. 5:17) is a victory only in principle,
then freedom exists only in principle, not in reality. Although
its mission (Phil. 2:16) demanded that a community be 'in the
world', it had to strive not to 'belong to the world' (Col. 2:20).
Any failure would make it vulnerable to Satan (2:11).

Paul's sudden shift from the situation at Corinth to his move from Troas to Macedonia is not really as abrupt as it at first seems. It is a way of articulating his love for the Corinthians. He was so desperately anxious to have news of them from Titus, the bearer of the Sorrowful Letter, that he gave up a successful ministry in Troas to set out on the road to meet him (2:12–13).

CHAPTER 4

Authentic ministry (2:14–6:10)

This section is the heart of Letter A. Despite the reconciliation that Paul has just celebrated in the previous section,
there was still some unfinished business that touched the
very core of his being. For him to be a Christian was to be an
apostle, and the authenticity of his ministry had been challenged. Even if he believed that the voices that spoke against
him had been stilled by love, the questions they had asked
needed to be answered if the future of the community was to
be assured.

From one point of view his response is very unsatisfactory.
He rambles from one theme to another, turns aside, back-
tracks and goes round in circles. There is no clear, logical
development from one point to another until a water-tight
case has been built up. This is certainly not because Paul
was incapable of writing in this way. His treatment of the
resurrection in 1 Corinthians 15 proves the opposite. If he
did not adopt such a didactic approach here, it was because
he felt that something else was required.

In fact, he is trying to do three things at once: to reply to
objections; to wean the Spirit-people from the Judaizers; and
to present his gospel in a form palatable to the Spirit-people.
Inevitably, therefore, he slides from one objective to another
and back again. He is deliberately trying to be subtle and
does not push any one point too hard. Behind the tactics,
however, lies a very clear and profound vision of authentic
ministry, which is striking in its Christological intensity.

MINISTRY: THEORY AND PRACTICE (2:14–3:6)

For a number of scholars this section belongs to a letter distinct from that to which the preceding section belongs, because they cannot see any connection between the mention of Paul's move to Macedonia and the theoretical discussion which he initiates here. The connection is not logical but associative. The mention of Macedonia triggered in Paul's mind a memory of the Macedonian churches at Philippi and Thessalonica, which were apostolic in precisely the same sense as he conceived his own ministry. By the quality of their community life the Philippians 'held forth the word of life' (Phil. 2:16), and of the Thessalonians he said 'Not only has the word of the Lord sounded forth from you in Macedonia and Achaia, but your faith in God has gone forth everywhere, so that we need not say anything' (1 Thess. 1:8). They had so integrated the message of Paul's gospel that they became a living *kerygma*. Very naturally, then, Paul's mind moved to a consideration of the nature of proclamation. This also explains the shift from the first-person singular (2:12–13) to the first-person plural (2:14–17). He was thinking not merely of himself and his immediate collaborators, but also of those communities whose 'life' was a proclamation which prolonged and extended his efforts.

This spread of the gospel was for Paul a resounding event in world history, and it brought to his mind the image that dominates 2:14–16. Despite obvious political overtones, a Roman triumph was essentially a religious act. The processions of the victorious general, accompanied by his troops, spoils and captives, culminated with sacrifices at the temple of Jupiter to honour the god who had granted the victory. Contrary to what might be expected, Paul does not depict himself as the victorious general – that role he reserves to God. Paul presents himself as one of the captives destined to be executed (2:14a).[21] This is consonant with what he says later:

---

[21] At least ten different interpretations have been suggested for *triambeuein* in order to bring the image into line with the expectations of exegetes. S. J. Hafemann has shown that 'The use of *triambeuein* with prepositional phrases to indicate its object or with a direct object alone, always refers to the one having been conquered and subsequently led in the procession, and never to the one having conquered, or to

'while we live we are always being given up to death for Jesus' sake' (4:11); note the use of 'always' in both phrases. His ministry is characterized not by glory, but by suffering. In addition to all the physical dangers which he encounters, 'there is the daily pressure upon me of my anxiety for all the churches' (11:28). Such misery and deprivation cannot be an argument against the authority of his ministry (as the Spirit-people would have it) because it is willed by God; it is the means which He has chosen to spread the gospel. Paul's weakness demonstrates that the power he displays in founding communities originates with God (cf. 4:7; 12:9). If to all appearances he is incapable, he *must* function as a channel of divine power.

From one aspect of the triumph image, Paul then moves to another, that of sacrifice (2:14b–16) which, however, he interprets in specifically Jewish terms. In the LXX 'the aroma of a sweet smell' had become a technical phrase to denote a sacrifice acceptable to God (cf. Gen. 8:21; Ezek. 20:41; Sir. 35:5; 38:11). The sacrifice is the crucified Christ (2:15a), whose death is the foundation of salvation. Paul then presents himself as the aroma of this sacrifice. Those who could not see a sacrifice taking place became aware of it through the odour. Similarly those who did not know of Christ's sacrificial death became aware of it through Paul and his collaborators. The language implicitly identifies Paul and Christ, but this will not be explained until 4:10–11.

Those who hear Paul's message are divided into 'those being saved' and 'those who are perishing' (2:15b). The basis is not predestination, as if God had chosen some for salvation and others for damnation. Paul's assessment is based on whether they have accepted his preaching or not and is valid only for a precise moment in time. Those who have accepted are not saved; they are only in the process of being saved, and this process could be disrupted (cf. 1 Cor. 5:5; 10:12). Equally, those who today refuse his message might accept it tomorrow,

those who shared in his victory . . . And, as we have seen, this illustration often, or even normally culminated, as did the procession as a whole, with the execution of these prisoners (or a representative selection of them),' *Suffering and the Spirit. An Exegetical Study of II Cor. 2:14–3:3 within the Context of the Corinthian Correspondence* (WUNT 2, 19; Tubingen, 1986), 33.

but as long as they maintain their refusal they are tarnished by the generic condemnation of sinful humanity (cf. Rom. 5:18).

The consequences of acceptance and refusal are articulated in terms of life and death (2:16a). Both can be understood physically (A), existentially (B) and eschatologically (C), as the following citation from Philo makes clear:

> I attended the lectures of a wise woman, whose name is Consideration, and was rid of my questioning; for she taught me that some people are dead [B] while living [A], and some alive [A] while dead [B]. She told me that bad people prolonging their days to extreme old age, are dead [B], deprived of the life [B] associated with virtue, while good people, even if cut off from their partnership with the body, live for ever [C] and are granted immortality. (*De Fuga*, 55)

Since they are physically alive, 'from death to death' can only mean from inauthentic existence to eschatological condemnation. The antithesis, 'from life to life', must, therefore, mean from authentic existence to eternal life.

This brings Paul to an awareness of his awesome responsibility. His ministry determines the fate of his hearers, not in the present, but for all eternity. His role is not merely existential but eschatological. The consequence is an abrupt change of tone: 'Who is competent for these things?' (2:16b). The question grows spontaneously out of what has been said, but it was also one which his opponents were asking. How should it be answered? Obviously, in the affirmative, as the following verse indicates. He has been commissioned by God, which guarantees his authority; he speaks before God, which guarantees his truthfulness; and he speaks 'in Christ', that is, with the dependability of Christ (cf. 1:18–22).[22]

This answer, of course, left Paul open to the charge that he was praising himself (3:1). He was not prepared to take the defensive, but moves to the attack. In opposition to his own practice (1 Cor. 9:15–18), he points out that his adversaries

---

[22] Dunn has suggested that 'in Christ' here (and in 5:17; 12:19) 'expresses not merely a rational conviction, but something more – a sense that Christ is thoroughly involved in the situation or action in question – *a consciousness of Christ*'. (*Jesus and the Spirit. A Study of the Religious and Charismatic Experience of Jesus and the First Christians as Reflected in the New Testament* (Philadelphia, 1975), 324). In each case, however, a specific nuance must be derived from the situation or action.

take money for preaching (2:17a). The (probably unfair) implication is that they do it for the money, not like Paul, who feels that he has no choice. He finds another weakness in the fact that they came to Corinth with letters of recommendation (3:1b). They should rather highlight results, as Paul does by claiming the Corinthian community as his letter of recommendation (3:2).[23] The very existence of the community affirmed the power and authority of Paul. The quality of its communal life was a message to the world advertising the effects of grace (cf. 1 Thess. 1:8; Phil. 2:16).

Paul then goes on to claim that his letter of recommendation is not only different in kind, but was issued by a much higher authority: namely, Christ (3:3a). The underlying idea once again is that the community is the continuing actualization in history of the ministry of Christ, but Paul moves away very quickly because he cannot say that Christ 'wrote' the letter, and so he returns to the nature of the letter. One would have expected him to say that it was 'written not with ink . . ., not on parchment', since this is the natural contrast with the letters brought by his adversaries. If he introduces the idea of 'tablets of stone' (3:3b) it can only be because he associated the bearers of the letters of recommendation with the Mosaic Law. On Mount Sinai Moses received 'the two tablets of testimony, tablets of stone written with the finger of God' (Exod. 24:12; 31:18). The intruders therefore were Judaizers.

Further confirmation of this identification is furnished by the following verses, where Paul formally answers the question he posed in 2:16b. Of himself, he is not competent to carry out the ministry he exercises: 'Our competency is not from ourselves' and 'we do not reckon anything as coming from ourselves' (3:5a). On the contrary, 'Our competency is from God, who has made us competent to be ministers of a new covenant not of the letter but of the spirit' (3:5b–6a). The distinction implicit in this formulation is best brought out by

---

23 C. K. Barrett (*The Second Epistle to the Corinthians* (BNTC; London, 1973), 96) rightly prefers the reading 'written in *your* hearts' (3:2), even though it is weakly attested. The alternative 'in *our* hearts' is nonsense, despite its overwhelming support among commentators. The 'heart' is understood as the source of all human activity.

the paraphrase, 'we are not letter-ministers but spirit-ministers of the new covenant'.[24]

The only reason why Paul would speak in this way is that his opponents were claiming to be 'ministers of the new covenant'. Why Judaizers should have adopted this title is clear from Jeremiah, who wrote, 'Behold the days are coming, says the Lord, when I will make a new covenant with the house of Israel and the house of Judah . . . This is my covenant which I will make with the house of Israel. After those days, says the Lord, I will adapt my laws to their understanding and write them on their hearts, and I will be their God and they will be my people' (31:31–3). The mention of 'laws' permitted them to maintain the enduring validity of the Mosaic Law, while at the same time recognizing that the eschaton had been inaugurated in Christ. Paul's experience of Judaism *as lived* (Phil. 3:6) had convinced him that if the Law were given any role in a religious community it tended to become central and to push God's gracious choice and mercy (theoretically the fundamental elements of Judaism) to the unconsidered periphery of human life. He had seen this happen in the church of Antioch (Gal. 2:11–21), and he was determined that it should not occur in his churches. He could not, however, simply repudiate the new covenant concept that appeared to legitimize his opponents' approach, because it formed part of the Words of Institution that he had transmitted to the Corinthians (1 Cor. 11:23–5). Hence, he was forced to introduce the distinction between a letter-vision and a spirit-vision of the new covenant, and to insist that attention to the letter of the Law meant existential 'death', whereas existential 'life' is given exclusively by the spirit of God in Christ (cf. 2:17; 1 Cor. 15:45) to which believers respond in full freedom.

---

[24] Grammatically 'not of the letter but of the spirit' qualifies 'new covenant' and not 'covenant' alone (so, rightly, V. P. Furnish, *II Corinthians* (AB; Garden City, NY, 1984), 199). Paul is distinguishing between two forms of 'new covenant', not between an old covenant of the letter and a new covenant of the spirit.

MINISTRY: OLD AND NEW (3:7–4:6)

Having refused the basic premise of the Judaizers (3:1–6), Paul now turns to the most troubling aspect of their presence at Corinth, the alliance they had formed with the Spirit-people. His basic concern in this section is to attract the Spirit-people to his side, and to achieve this he developed a subtle two-pronged attack. On one hand, his reformulation of the gospel is calculated both to harmonize with, and delicately but firmly to refashion the Philonic perspective which the Spirit-people had received from Apollos. On the other hand, he presents the message of the Judaizers in such a way as to make it as unpalatable as possible to those who prided themselves as being in the forefront of religious thought.[25]

The salient feature of the first part of this section is the prominence given to Moses. This is without parallel in any other Pauline letter, and must be explained by something in the situation at Corinth.[26] What this was can only be a matter of speculation, but the hypothesis that does full justice to the data is that the Spirit-people were comparing Paul unfavourably with Moses. The Judaizers, of course, had highlighted Moses as the great Law-giver, and the Spirit-people probably developed this in a Philonic perspective. Moses for them was

[25] Some scholars believe that in 3:7–18 Paul is merely exploiting the virtualities of the Old Testament without particular reference to the situation at Corinth: e.g. J. Fitzmyer, 'Glory Reflected on the Face of Christ (2 Cor. 3:7–4:6) and a Palestinian Jewish Motif', *TS* 42 (1981), 630–44; and most recently F. Young and D. F. Ford, *Meaning and Truth in 2 Corinthians* (London, 1987), 83. Others maintain that Paul is quoting and correcting an interpretation of Exodus 34 put forward by his opponents: e.g. D. Georgi, *The Opponents of Paul in Second Corinthians* (Philadelphia, 1986), 264–71. The former do not respect the polemic dimension of this section, and the reconstructions of the latter are based on a flawed methodology. The position adopted here is explained in more detail in my '*Pneumatikoi* and Judaizers in 2 Cor. 2:14–4:6', *AusBR* 34 (1986), 42–58.

[26] To say that 'Moses is the figure on which Paul's ministry is modelled' or 'Clearly Moses is the "type" or "model" of Paul's role' (Young and Ford, *Meaning and Truth*, 82) is a radical misunderstanding. Paul modelled his ministry on that of Jesus Christ (1 Cor. 11:1; 2 Cor. 4:10–11).

the epitome of Hellenistic virtues and thus clothed with a radiance to which Paul could not aspire.[27]

There was but one text in the Old Testament which would permit him to refute such criticism in a form that would impress the Spirit-people, namely Moses' veiling of his face in Exodus 34:34–5, and the central point of his response is 3:12–13, to which we shall come in a moment.

This choice forced Paul to deal with the 'glory' of Moses. Thus, he begins with an allusion to Exodus 34:29 which uses the reaction of the Israelites to highlight the brightness of Moses' countenance (3:7b). Such a vision of Moses, of course, worked against him, but Paul cleverly turns it to his advantage by using a rabbinic argument called 'from the lesser to the greater'. In syllogistic terms this can be expressed in the form: A is greater than B, but B enjoys quality X; therefore A enjoys this quality in greater measure than B. Obviously, such an argument proves nothing regarding the real relationship of A to B. It works only for those already committed to the major premise, and the Corinthians were, of course, Christians.

Thus Paul describes the Christian ministry as superior to the Mosaic ministry (notice that he has abandoned the word 'covenant') in terms of glory in three different ways. First he contrasts the ministry of 'death' with that of 'spirit' (3:7–8), and then with a slight variation the ministry of 'condemnation' with that of 'righteousness' (3:9). In the process he identifies the Law as effecting a condemnation leading to existential death, and claims 'spirit' (which would have pleased the Spirit-people) and 'righteousness' (which would have annoyed the Judaizers) for his own ministry. Christ is identified with righteousness and sanctification in 1 Corinthians 1:30. The third argument is the most important because he there contrasts the 'transitory' (Law) with the 'permanent' (gospel). Here again Paul is speaking from a specifically Christian perspective. Since the Law has given way to the gospel, the role of the former in God's plan can only have been provisional and

---

[27] Philo wrote of Moses, 'those who saw him were filled with awe and amazement; nor even could their eyes continue to stand the dazzling that flashed from him like the rays of the sun' (*Vita Moysis* 2:70).

preparatory. Its function, ended with Christ (Rom. 10:4). Paul's awareness of the faith perspective underlying his arguments is clear in 3:12a. Absolutely speaking, the Christian dispensation might be only another transitory phase in God's dealings with humanity. His assessment that it was the last and permanent phase enjoyed only the certitude of hope.

The kernel of Paul's response to his critics is the contrast he establishes between his behaviour and that of Moses (3:12–13). This is expressed in terms of *parrhesia*, which connotes 'confident openness' in both the political and moral spheres.[28] It had special importance in the writings of Philo where it is the essential property of noble souls fortified by virtue (*Probus*, 150–2); as the fruit of wisdom it implies friendship with God (*Heres*, 14–21). Since Moses disguised the residual traces of God's glory by hiding his face, he cannot have possessed the quality of 'confident openness', and in consequence he must have lacked all the other virtues associated with it. Paul, on the contrary, never tried to be other than he really was. He exhibited the 'confident openness' which characterizes the truly wise and noble soul. Thus, very neatly and with great economy of words, Paul establishes his superiority to Moses in a way precisely calculated to appeal to the Spirit-people. And the Judaizers could not deny his premise because the fact of Moses' dissimulation was attested by their sacred text (Exod. 34:34–5).

Paul's next stop is to associate Moses' achievement with intellectual blindness and an out-of-date religious message. The Judaizers had played into his hands by introducing the idea of a new covenant, because this enabled him to stigmatize the Law as the *old* covenant (3:14). By using 'Moses' alone (3:15) instead of 'the book of Moses' (2 Chr. 35:12) or 'the book of the covenant' (2 Chr. 34:40), he cleverly attaches to the figure of Moses the pejorative connotation of 'old'. Whatever role he had in the history of salvation has now been superseded. The minds and hearts of his followers were 'veiled' because they failed to perceive the significance of the fading glory of Moses' face. Their intellectual blindness was manifest

28 S. B. Marrow, '*Parrhēsia* and the New Testament', *CBQ* 44 (1982), 431–46.

in that they gave a permanent value to something that was essentially provisional and temporary, and this continues in the synagogue to the present day (3:14).

Paul pursues his tactic of making the Law as unattractive as possible to the avant-garde Spirit-people by a subtle adaptation of Exodus 34:34, 'when anyone turns to the Lord, the veil is removed' (3:16), which furnishes him with a simple and effective *ad hominem* argument. In the Corinthian community there were Jews (Acts 18:8) who had turned to Christ (3:14). Their conversion implied that they had found something lacking in their previous mode of life based on the Law. They had been blind but now they see. Why then, Paul implies, would the Spirit-people want to commit themselves to the darkness of intellectual sclerosis when they could have the light of authentic glory?

Without losing sight of his objective of trying to wean the Spirit-people from the Judaizers, Paul now attempts to seduce them by appropriating two key words from their lexicon, namely, 'spirit' and 'freedom' (3:17). By asserting that 'the Lord' of 3:16 is 'the spirit', he identifies the Lord to whom believers turn at their conversion as the God of that new covenant which he has characterized as being of the 'spirit' and not of the 'letter' (3:6). God may once have spoken through the letter of the Law, but he does so no longer. He now acts in history through the Spirit to produce 'life' and righteousness (3:7–9). Since the human person is a decision-making being, righteousness, which is authentic 'life', cannot be given. It must be chosen in freedom. Thus, 'life' is impossible for those who consider themselves *bound* by the Law; they condemn themselves to existential 'death' (3:7–9).

The point here is not that the content of the Law is erroneous. On the contrary, Paul insists that it is holy and just and good (Rom. 7:12). What he is criticizing is an attitude of such total respect that the law is given complete blind obedience. When the Law is accorded absolute authority and humanity feels constrained to accept its dictates, the purpose of the Law is distorted (cf. Rom. 7:10) and humanity corrupted. The Law was given to guide humanity (Gal. 3:24). It was there to be used, and Paul did, but he did not permit himself to be used by it, as were the Judaizers.

The resonances of 'spirit' for the Spirit-people hardly need emphasis. It was the form in which they had appropriated for themselves the Philonic category of the heavenly man, i.e. the ideal model of authentic humanity. The theme of freedom was so central to Philo's thought that he devoted a whole book to *Every Good Man is Free*, according to which the free are the virtuous, the perfect and above all the wise. Freedom, therefore, is the concomitant of *parrhesia* 'confident openness' (3:12), for both are rooted in the same virtues. Paul very delicately insinuates that the gospel is identified with the virtues which the Spirit-people esteemed most highly.

By highlighting the consequences of the conversion to Christianity evoked in 3:16, this approach is further developed. By using the phrase 'with unveiled face' (3:18a) Paul intends both to compare and contrast believers with Moses. The contrast with 3:13 indicates that they have the 'confident openness' which Moses lacked, and in consequence possess the freedom given by the Spirit (3:17). But Moses was not always veiled: 'Whenever Moses went in before the Lord to speak to him he removed the veil' (Exod. 34:34). Like Moses, therefore, Christians have privileged access to God, and in this they are contrasted with the 'veiled ones' whose concern is the text of the Law. Paul plays on the admiration of the Spirit-people for Moses 'the all wise', while at the same time introducing a subtle note of criticism of the Judaizers.

The text of Exodus just cited gives the impression that Moses had direct access to God. Paul reacts against this view in writing 'we behold as in a mirror the glory of God' (3:18b), a formulation which again implicitly contrasts Christians with the followers of Moses, who had access only to *his* glory. Paul's principle concern, however, is to introduce the idea of mediation, because he had to bring the Spirit-people to a correct appreciation of the role of Christ.

In line with Philo's teaching, the Spirit-people believed that their access to God was through Wisdom. In 1 Corinthians Paul corrected this view by identifying the historical Jesus as the true wisdom of God (1:24, 30). He here does the same thing, but in a way better calculated to appeal to the Spirit-people, and without compromising his own convictions: 'We are all being transformed into the same image from glory to glory' (3:18c). Philo's doctrine of the 'Image' would have been familiar to anyone acquainted with his teaching. Particularly relevant here is his view that 'the Image becomes the pattern of all other beings' (*Legum Allegoriarum* 3:96), which, of course, is a reference to creation. This theme is taken up by Paul, who transposes it to highlight the goal of the new creation, which is achieved through progressive transformation.

There was a widespread Hellenistic belief that the vision of a god or goddess had a transforming effect on the spectator.[29] These stories were so much part of the popular culture that it would have been natural for the Spirit-people to think of the glory of Moses as a 'transformation'. Paul had already introduced an element of doubt into their understanding of this transformation by insisting that it had been merely transitory (3:7, 13). In now claiming an ever-intensifying transformation for believers, he achieves a description of the effects of the gospel that would have been both flattering and intelligible to the Spirit-people.[30]

But there must be no misunderstanding. Believers are not transformed into gods, but are progressively conformed to Christ. The discreet allusion to Christ ('the same image'; cf. 4:4) deepens the hint at the end of 3:14, and at the same time facilitates a subtle modification of the concept of 'glory'. Christ is glorious as the visible manifestation of God's power and wisdom (1 Cor. 1:24). Since Paul refers to 'the glory of God on the face of Christ' (4:6), it must be understood that he had in mind a visible brightness similar to that which appeared on the face of Moses (3:7) but superior to it in terms of permanence (3:10–11). Since it is a question not of the face, but of the being

---

[29] For details see J. Behm, 'Metamorphoō' *TDNT* 4, 756–7.

[30] By the words *hemeis de pantes* 'we all' (3:18a; contrast 3:12) Paul broadens his perspective to include all believers in order to remind them that while God acts through the Spirit, the effect of his action is ever to produce the image of Jesus. In consequence, conformity to Jesus is the criterion by which the authenticity of the Spirit's action can be tested (cf. Dunn, *Jesus and the Spirit*, 320).

of believers, it is clear that their glory ('from glory to glory') cannot be interpreted in this way. Paul did not intend to speak of physical transformation of believers.

As applied to human beings 'glory of God' implies the ability to give glory to God, and is the equivalent of righteousness (cf. Rom. 3:23). 'From glory to glory', therefore, means that the goal of transformation is an increasing capacity to give glory to God. Since for Paul this is essentially an existence penetrated and informed by love (1 Cor. 13), believers are perceptively different from unbelievers, even though they lack the radiance of Moses (3:7) or Christ (4:6). This visible difference is the basis of Paul's theology of witness, which will be dealt with explicitly in 4:10–11. To culminate with a hint of the Christ-like behaviour expected of believers is typical of Paul's approach to the Spirit-people, because in an earlier letter he had argued that their comportment betrayed their lack of the wisdom they claimed (1 Cor. 3:1–4). But the overt criticism of that response is absent here, where the Spirit-people are invited to read between the lines.

The discipline, delicacy and tact displayed in 3:7–18 were too good to last. Paul could be subtle for only so long, and in 4:1–6 he returns to the forthright approach to his opponents which he displayed in 3:1–6. The two sections, in fact, have many contacts in style and content.

As in 2:17 he begins with the assertion that it is God who chose and empowered him for his ministry (4:1). To those who knew something of his career his use of the word 'mercy' would have been particularly evocative. He had been a persecutor of the church and it had taken a specific divine action in his regard to transform him into an apostle (1 Cor. 15:8–10; Gal. 1:11–16). The only response to such generosity is total dedication, and so in the face of dangers and difficulties that would make others 'shrink back' Paul goes forward with courageous openness and confidence (3:12).

One difficulty which complicated his life was criticism from those whom he had tried to help. His response is to insist that he never did anything of which he need be ashamed (4:2); in particular he never did anything underhand, nor did he tamper with the word of God. What he has in mind here can only be deduced from the corresponding positive statement that he always manifested the truth (4:2b). In the section 2:14–6:10 'to manifest' or its cognates appear seven times and in five of these the context highlights Christ (2:14; 3:3; 4:10–11; 5:10). The statistics suggest that 'full disclosure' was an issue at Corinth and that the subject of the debate was Christ. His opponents were misrepresenting the real nature of the gospel by failing to highlight the essential role of Christ. This was true both of the Spirit-people and of the Judaizers: the latter by presenting the Law as a means of salvation reduced the contribution of Christ to insignificance; the former, if they considered Christ at all, thought of him as the Lord of glory in a way that divorced him entirely from the crucified Jesus (1 Cor. 2:8). For Paul, Jesus was the truth of Christ (Eph. 4:20–1),[31] and at Corinth he had proclaimed 'I decided to know nothing among you except Jesus Christ and him crucified' (1 Cor. 2:2). Such openness should commend him to all capable of an objective judgement.

At Corinth, on the contrary, it gave rise to the objection that his gospel was 'veiled' (4:3). It was argued that Paul's gospel had won few converts because of his unimpressive personality and lacklustre preaching (cf. 10:10). He was not a dominant figure, whose words were of commanding eloquence and grandeur. Such criticism is likely to have come from the Spirit-people, who would have compared him unfavourably with Apollos. In their view he would have had a wider appeal and enjoyed greater success had he adopted the sophisticated approach of his Alexandrian co-worker.

The form of Paul's response is very curious, because he embarks on a little disquisition on those outside the church (4:4), even though the criticism has come from believers. The tactic can work only if we assume that he is setting up a situation with which he expects his opponents to identify, and in consequence correct themselves. This again is a pointer to

---

[31] See I. de la Potterie, 'Jésus et la verité d'après Eph. 4.21', *Studiorum Paulinorum Congressus Internationalis Catholicus, II* (AnBib 18; Rome, 1963), 45–57.

the Spirit-people because from 1 Corinthians Paul had learnt that they reacted very badly to direct criticism.

'The god of this age' (4:4) is commonly identified with Satan, but this is certainly wrong, because in Pauline usage Satan is exclusively the enemy of believers. Beliar (6:16) is a more likely candidate, but even this identification should not be accepted too readily. Would so thorough-going a monotheist as Paul have predicated 'god' of an evil spirit? Particularly since in 1 Corinthians 8:5 he is careful to refer to 'so-called gods'. On the contrary, the genitive of content is common in the Pauline letters, and in this case one would translate 'the god who is this age'; compare 'their god is their belly' (Phil. 3:19). In Paul's lexicon 'this age' is a synonym for 'this world'. How relevant this interpretation is to the context becomes apparent once it is recalled that the Spirit-people were applying to Paul the criteria by which their pagan contemporaries judged orators of all types. By implication, Paul is saying that they have become slaves to the conventions of the world, and as such are equivalent to unbelievers. This interpretation is confirmed by his use of the verb 'to blind', because for Philo 'blindness' characterized the attitude of those who were preoccupied with the externals of transient created things (*Heres*, 76–8).

The formulation 'the gospel of the glory of Christ' (4:4b) is also significant because it is unique in the letters and only one text offers a parallel in substance, 'None of the rulers of this age [compare: "god of this age"] understood this, for if they had they would not have crucified the Lord of glory' (1 Cor. 2:8). There Paul is criticizing the Spirit-people who in their wisdom were in danger of separating Christ from the cross. Here he is doing basically the same thing. The 'glory of Christ' is attained, not by wisdom, but in and through the gospel, which Paul preached in its full authenticity.

From the Spirit-people Paul's thought moves to their allies, the Judaizers (4:5). They preached themselves by vaunting their superior apostolic credentials (10:12; 11:5; 18; 12:11), and dominated the community by their demands (11:19–20). Neither Paul's simple statements of his call by God (2:17; 4:1) nor his presentation of himself as a model of authentic response to the gospel (1 Cor. 4:17; 11:1) can be construed as self-proclamation. His preaching was focused exclusively on Christ (1 Cor. 2:2), and it is this that made him a servant of the community: 'What is Apollos, what is Paul? Servants through whom you believed, as the Lord assigned to each' (1 Cor. 3:5). Paul has defined his attitude towards the Corinthians very precisely, 'We do not lord it over your faith, rather we are co-workers for your joy' (1:24). His role model in this has been the historical Jesus, whose total dedication to the service of others even to the point of dying for them is the standard of authentic human behaviour (5:15).

The contempt in which Paul held what he considered to be the self-serving ministry of the Judaizers sparked a reaction that gave birth to the sublime statement of his understanding of his own role, which concludes this section (4:6). Each element in the formulation has a parallel in 4:4 and his intention is obviously to present himself as the antithesis of those whom he has there criticized.

He identifies God as the one who said 'Out of darkness light shall shine' (4:6a). This is not an allusion to Genesis 1:3, but a combination of Job 37:15 ('he made light *out of darkness*'), which is a reflection on Genesis, and Isaiah 9:2 ('on you who dwell in the shadow of death a *light shall shine*'), which evokes the inbreaking of the eschaton. The God who brought the world into being is the one who decides the inauguration of the end time (Matt. 24:36). Contrary to the Jewish expectation of a great light surrounding Jerusalem, 'the glory of the Lord has risen upon you' (Isa. 60:1), the eschatological light is the radiance of glory on the face of Christ (4:6c). In him the pristine clarity of humanity as the image of God (Gen. 1:26–7) is restored (4:4d). He is the New Adam (1 Cor. 15:45), whose being is constituted by the creative love (1 Cor. 13:2) which is the nature of God (cf. 1 John 4:8, 16).

The light of this personality burst into the darkness enshrouding humanity, and into the heart of Paul at the moment of his conversion. In the present his weakness is the context of God's glory as he diffuses the knowledge of the definitive act of

God in Christ (2:14). His is not the striking brilliance which Moses exhibited on Sinai, but a personality aflame with love (2:4) who walks the road of suffering and death as another Christ.

MINISTRY AND MORTALITY (4:7–5:10)

The Spirit-people at Corinth were disconcerted by Paul. They wanted a leader whom they could admire and respect, and in whose power and presence they could take pride. He, however, exhibited none of the qualities they desired. In addition to his unimpressive personality and poor preaching his life was charcterized by failures, setbacks and suffering. How could such a person be God's agent in the salvation of humanity? This is the question which Paul now struggles to answer. He had already done so briefly in 1 Corinthians 1:18–31, where his point is that 'God made foolish the wisdom of the world' (1:20) by refusing to respect its scale of values, but he here goes into the matter much more deeply. Basically he deals with two issues: the relationship between suffering and ministry, and the prospect of death.

The manifestation of Jesus (4:7–15)

Paul begins with a very direct answer to the objection of the Spirit-people. God chooses agents who will make it evident that the power which brings the 'dead' to 'life' (2:16) is not theirs but his. The minister is like an 'earthen pot': cheap, fragile, expendable, unreparable (4:7). The image would have been natural to any reader of the Old Testament. If humanity was made from dust (Gen. 2:7), it was inevitable that God should be thought of as a potter (Isa. 29:16; 45:9; 64:8) and the human person as a pot; the destruction of the wicked is presented as the breaking of a pot (Isa. 30:14; Jer. 18:1–11; 19:1–13). The trifling value of the pot is contrasted with the 'treasure' it contains. The two do not belong together by nature. Someone must have placed the treasure in the pot. Equally, the 'surpassing power' displayed by the minister cannot originate in the fragility and vulnerability of his person; it must come from a higher source.

Paul then goes on to demonstrate that it is, in fact, a question of a 'surpassing power'. This he does by means of a 'catalogue of hardships' (4:8–9).[32] When compared with similar lists elsewhere in his letters (1 Cor. 4:9–13; 2 Cor. 6:4–5; 11:23–9; 12:10; Rom. 8:35), this catalogue stands out as unique. In each case, what is denied in the second member is the usual concomitant of the first. In other words, his reaction to suffering is not the normal one, and so demands an explanation, which can only be that he is aided by a miraculous power. Another aspect of this list appears when it is translated in such a way as to bring out the unity of the underlying image:

> pressed hard, but not driven into a corner;
> despairing, but not utterly desperate;
> pursued, but not abandoned;
> thrown down, but not defeated.

Paul is thinking of himself as a wrestler at grips with a more skilled opponent. The image was suggested by the 'earthen pot' and is a good example of how his mind works. Before a bout wrestlers oiled their bodies. When they got to grips sweat mixed with the oil, and so after a number of falls on the soft floor of the ring their bodies became encrusted with clay to the point where they looked like clay statues, men made of the same material as cheap household vessels.[33]

The divine power that enables Paul to survive all difficulties and dangers also transforms his being (4:10–11). This is his most profound statement on ministerial witness, and in order to understand it one must keep in mind the three senses of life and death explained on p. 31. The extraordinary first phrase

---

[32] Such catalogues were common in the ancient world. The comparative material is conveniently assembled in J. T. Fitzgerald, *Cracks in an Earthen Vessel. An Examination of the Catalogues of Hardships in the Corinthian Correspondence* (SBLDS 99; Atlanta, 1988).

[33] This interpretation proposed by C. Spicq ('L'Image sportive de 2 Cor 4:7–9', *ETL* 13 (1937), 209–29) has been contested by V. Pfitzner (*Paul and the Agon Motif. Traditional Athletic Imagery in the Pauline Literature* (NovTSup 17; Leiden, 1967), 76, note 1), but it remains the only unified hypothesis capable of explaining the series of pairs.

'carrying in the body the dying of Jesus'[34] (4:10a) is clarified by 'while we live we are always being given up to death on account of Jesus' (4:11a). In both clauses 'life' and 'death' are used in the normal physical sense. As long as he is alive Paul is in danger of death from persecution; he is 'in peril every hour' (1 Cor. 5:30). Yet he persists 'on account of Jesus', not only because he has been called, but because he has been inspired and challenged by the ministry of Jesus. When Paul uses Jesus without any other qualification (e.g. Lord, Christ) he means the earthly Jesus as distinguished from the risen Christ. The historical Jesus saw his death as the saving event whereby his ministry would be accomplished (cf. Luke 9:31). In his sense his whole ministry was a 'dying', a being given over to death. Paul viewed his own existence in the same perspective. His acceptance of suffering on account of Jesus meant that his physical being was marked by 'the dying of Jesus'.

It is a typical Pauline paradox that 'dying' should manifest 'life'. He accepts continuous threats to his physical existence 'in order that the life of Jesus may be manifested in our bodies [4:10b], in our mortal flesh' (4:11b). The stress on the fleshly body is important. Paul is talking about witness, which is a matter of sense perception, not about a verbal account of the earthly ministry of Jesus. It is a question of being something which can be seen, not of saying something to be heard. What, then, does the 'life of Jesus' mean?

Obviously 'life' is not used in the physical sense, because Paul is speaking of a present reality and Jesus was physically dead. The choice, therefore, is between the existential and eschatological senses. The majority of scholars opt for the latter, but a close reading of their explanations reveals that they understand the 'life of Jesus' as the 'power of the Risen

---

34 *Necrosis* is not attested prior to Paul's use here. If in Romans 4:19 it means 'a death-like state', the context here clearly indicates a process; hence 'dying' rather than 'death'. Some commentators give it a more objective cast, 'putting to death' (A. Plummer, *A Critical and Exegetical Commentary on the Second Epistle of St Paul to the Corinthians* (ICC; Edinburgh, 1915), 129), 'killing' (Barrett, *2 Corinthians*, 139). The striking similarity of the structure of this verse (4:10a) and that of Galatians 6:17 ('I bear in my body the marks of Jesus') suggests that, in using 'Jesus' unqualified, Paul is thinking specifically of the earthly Jesus, as is also the case in the bracketing texts 2 Corinthians 4:5b and 4:14.

Christ'.[35] If this is what Paul in fact means, why does he not say so more directly? Moreover, these commentators do not respect the specific connotation of 'Jesus' or give due weight to the stress on the physical dimension. Hence, it is preferable to understand 'life' in the existential sense, i.e. as a mode of human existence (cf. Rom. 6:13), which has been perfectly defined by Philo as loving God and living for him alone (*De Posteritate Caini*, 69; *De Mutatione Nominum*, 213). This is certainly an accurate description of the consistent attitude both of the historical Jesus and of Paul. It is in this sense that the latter can present his comportment as manifesting the 'life of Jesus'. The identity is functional, not ontological. Paul continues to demonstrate the real possibiity of a mode of existence which was once revealed in the historical Jesus.

The importance of this for Paul derives from his understanding of humanity as enslaved to Sin (Rom. 3:9; 6:6, 17, 20; Gal. 3:22). Those born into society find themselves in the grip of a false value system. Their pattern of behaviour is determined by the lived inauthentic values that they see all around them. In order to restore choice, which is fundamental to the decision of faith, God sent his Son (Rom. 8:3), who in his comportment exhibited an alternative value system. Inauthenticity was now confronted with authenticity. Grace stood in visible contrast to Sin. Paul was convinced that it had to remain so. Authenticity had to be demonstrated, not merely talked about. Verbal preaching had to be backed up by the existential proclamation of 'the life of Jesus' in a pattern of behaviour which manifested the effects of grace. Only thus could the alternative introduced into history by Jesus be preserved. Humanity had to be *shown* that the mode of being exhibited by Jesus was still really

---

[35] See in particular, Barrett, *2 Corinthians*, 140 and Furnish, *II Corinthians*, 283. This would also appear to be Dunn's opinion since he accepts the New English Bible translation of *he zoe tou Iesou*, 'the life that Jesus lives' (*Jesus and the Spirit*, 333). This interpretation has been convincingly demolished by Georgi who, however, then goes on to claim that 'the life of Jesus' was a slogan of Paul's opponents, for whom it signified 'the sensational power of life demonstrated by the *theios aner* Jesus in the past, which could be reproduced by his messengers in the present' (*Opponents of Paul*, 275). In fact, Paul's adversaries focused on the Lord of Glory (1 Cor. 2:8) to the detriment of the historical Jesus (1 Cor. 12:3; 2 Cor. 11:4), which forced the apostle to emphasize the reality of suffering and death in the life of Jesus.

possible, if the gospel is to be heard in a way that makes faith feasible.[36]

The interpretation which Paul has just given of the relation of his sufferings to his ministry is based on faith. He believes, as did the writer of Psalms (LXX), that his perseverance, despite deprivations and setbacks, is due to God's grace, and that his dedication shows forth 'the life of Jesus'. He cannot produce any rational proof of the truth of such statements. He emphasizes the faith element (4:13), however, not in order to stress the obvious, but to insinuate that the Spirit-people should have 'the spirit which is faith'. They prided themselves on such gifts of the Spirit as speaking in tongues (1 Cor. 14). They should rather cultivate the gift of faith that would permit them to penetrate beyond externals to the reality of Gods plan (cf. 4:18; 5:12; 11:18). Since Paul's comportment is based on faith they can understand him only if they too have faith.

At first sight, it is curious that Paul should then go on to talk about resurrection (4:14). It becomes understandable only if we recall that he has said 'Death is at work in us, but life in you' (4:12). 'Death' here must be understood in the physical sense: Paul is being ground down by persecution and pressures of all sorts (4:16), in order to bring the gift of 'life' in the existential sense to the Corinthians (4 Gal. 4:19). This is why Paul has to be 'raised' whereas the Corinthians do not; contrast 1 Corinthians 6:14; Romans 8:11. He uses resurrection language metaphorically, as in 13:4, to evoke a return visit to Corinth.[37] Once he has been reunited with the community, with whom he has just been reconciled (7:7), they will stand before the world as those whom the power of God has brought from 'death' to 'life' (Rom. 6:13). Such existential witness is a 'holding forth of the word of life' (Phil. 2:16), and through it grace will reach out to touch ever more people, with

---

[36] This missionary dimension of Paul's thought is not adequately respected by Dunn, who treats 4:7–12 rather abstractly in terms of the meaning of suffering (*Jesus and the Spirit*, 327–8).

[37] Detailed justification of this interpretation is given in my 'Faith and Resurrection in 2 Cor 4:13–14', *RB* 95 (1988), 543–50.

a consequent increase in the thanksgiving which glorifies God (4:15).

Facing the fear of death (4:16–5:10)

Having just defined suffering as 'death working in us' (4:12) it is very natural that Paul should now take up the logic of the meaning of physical death. He had been in situations where he was convinced that death was imminent (1:9; 11:25), and this is always an incentive to incisive reflection.

The contrast between 'outer man' and 'inner man' (4:16) should not be interpreted as functioning like the Greek dualism of body and soul, because such a dichotomy had no place in Paul's thought. As his teaching on resurrection indicates (1 Cor. 15), the body was an essential component of the person. In opposition to the Greeks, who saw the body as a prison from which the soul had to be liberated, he viewed the body as the only sphere in which the commitment of the spirit to Christ became real. The 'outer-man', therefore, is the visible dimension of human existence, and when Paul says that it is 'being disabled', he has in mind the ill effects which are the consequences of wounds, blows, illness and fatigue. New lines appear on his face; his limbs do not have the flexibility and resilience which they once had. The invisible dimension of human existence ('the inner man'), on the contrary, is 'being renewed every day' in the sense that his faith is continuously strengthened. He becomes ever more convinced that God has chosen him and that his mission is critical to the salvation of the human race. This is why he does not lose heart (4:16a).

This perspective, however, leaves a number of questions unanswered. Why does Paul's faith grow? What will happen when the body becomes so disabled that it can no longer respond to the commands of the spirit? Paul begins his response by contrasting present sufferings and future glory in terms of duration and weight (4:17). Suffering is momentary and light when compared with the eternity and weight of the glory reserved for the righteous in heaven. Paul is so confident of the goodness of God that he explicitly underlines that the reward will be out of all proportion to the contribution he makes in and through his deprivations. Thus there is no question of earning a reward; it is fundamentally God's gift prompted only by love.

This understanding of Paul's situation escaped the Spirit-people and the Judaizers because they focused on the 'things that are seen' (4:18). They judged Paul solely on externals. His trials and tribulations showed that he did not measure up to the standard they expected of a religious leader. In their wisdom, however, they should have known better. What is visible is subject to the normal law of decay; it is material and essentially transitory, and thus an unsatisfactory basis for any enduring assessment. The 'things that are unseen', known only by faith, by definition belong to another world. Spiritual realities are untouched by decay and consequently exist eternally. They, therefore, should be the basis of any truly wise judgement. Paul does not question the reality of the 'things that are seen', as Plato did, but their ultimate significance. The effect of sufferings is negated by the hope of the invisible (cf. Rom. 8:24).

Paul is not proposing a vision which legitimates suffering, as has often been the case in the western Christian tradition. This in essence amounts to turning someone else's cheek by a promise of pie in the sky. Paul's opposition to such an attitude is clear from his consistent stress on the primacy of charity: 'Without love I do not exist' (1 Cor. 13:2); 'Bear one another's burdens, and so fulfil the law of Christ' (Gal. 6:2). The very being of Christians consists in a power that reaches out to enable others in all spheres of life. Social ills, therefore, cannot be tolerated as a necessary form of asceticism. Paul, however, was not so naive as to believe that a new religious community could be established without persecution. The violent opposition which he had encountered would also threaten to overwhelm the churches he founded. This type of suffering had to be accepted by Christians. It was both a defence and means of spreading the gospel. Conviction which survives intense pressure excites respect and admiration. It is the existential witness which enables others to break the bonds of Sin by convincing them that another mode of life is both possible and desirable. In this sense all believers are apostles and, like Paul, should not be discouraged by suffering even if this should lead to death.

Death should not be feared because it is not the end of everything but a transition to another world (5:1-5).[38] Again, Paul does not prove this; he states it as an unquestioned axiom rooted in Jewish tradition. The fragility of earthly existence, where violence, accident or illness may strike at any moment, is symbolized by an 'earthly tent-like house' which is easily swept away. When this happens, Paul affirms with certitude, it will be replaced by an enduring dwelling in the heavens (5:1). The background of this language is to be found in texts such as 'In those days a whirlwind carried me off from the earth, and set me down at the end of the heavens, and there I saw another vision, the dwelling places of the holy ones [angels] and the resting places of the righteous' (1 Enoch 39:3-4), whose influence is also visible in the Fourth Gospel: 'In my Father's house there are many dwelling places; if there were not, would I have told you that I go to prepare a place for you' (John 14:2). There are many other such texts from the intertestamental period, and in all the building simply symbolizes the future sphere in which the just exist. The perspective is existential and not anthropological. The weight of this tradition is the most important clue as to the way 5:1-5 must be read. To say, as some have done, that the 'house not made with hands eternal in the heavens' represents the resurrection body is to introduce a specification alien to Paul's thought and irrelevant to his purpose. The point of 5:1 is to contrast the transitory character of present existence with the enduring character of future existence. The modality of either form is not the issue.

Paul longs for the security of heavenly existence, 'greatly

---

[38] A survey of 'the incredible multiplicity of opinions' is given by E.-B. Allo, *Saint Paul. Seconde Épître aux Corinthiens* (Paris, 1936), 137-55, and at much greater length by F. Land, *2 Korinther 5:1-10 in der neueren Forschung* (BGBE; Tubingen, 1973). The majority divorce the passage from its context and interpret the images anthropologically and individualistically. The defects of this approach have been convincingly exposed by Furnish, who persuasively argued that the context requires that the images be interpreted existentially (*II Corinthians*, 288-95; similarly Young and Ford, *Meaning and Truth*, 132-3).

desiring to clothe ourselves with our heavenly dwelling' (5:2).
The awful mixed metaphor becomes intelligible only when it is
recognized that garment symbolism appears as a synonym for
dwelling symbolism in the Jewish tradition which influenced
5:1, e.g. 'The righteous and the elect shall have risen from the
earth . . . and they shall have been clothed with garments of
glory, and these shall be the garments of life from the Lord of
spirits. And your garments shall not grow old, nor your glory
pass away before the Lord of spirits' (1 Enoch 62:15–16). 'To
clothe ourselves', however, does not render Paul's Greek
precisely. The literal meaning of the verb is 'to put on one
garment over another', and it betrays his expectation of being
alive at the *Parousia*, the second coming of Christ in glory,
which he will make explicit in 5:4.

He does not follow through with this idea immediately,
because he has just realized that he has been presuming that he
will end up in heaven, and that this might give the impression
that heaven was the automatic goal of human life. Hence, he
brings this assumption into the open in a brief parenthesis
(5:3), which complicates the understanding of his main point
because he uses the symbol of 'clothed' in a new sense. The
verse may be paraphrased as 'Presupposing, of course, that we
shall not be found guilty but righteous', and the necessity of
divine judgement is formally stated in 5:10. Due to the
influence of the idea of clothing in the previous verse, Paul
expresses guilt in terms of nakedness, which was common
among the prophets of the Old Testament, e.g. 'Your
nakedness shall be uncovered, and your shame shall be seen. I
will take vengeance and spare no one' (Isa. 47:3; cf. 20:2–4)
and 'I will deliver you into the hands of those whom you hate
. . . and they will leave you naked and bare and the nakedness
of your harlotry shall be uncovered (Ezek. 23:28–9). By
contrast 'clothed' came to have the sense of non-guilty. Thus
Jesus declares that admission to the messianic banquet is
conditional on having the appropriate garment (Matt. 22:11).
To be clothed, therefore, means a quality of moral life that God
will judge favourable, whereas in 5:2 it meant the mode of
being consequent on a favourable final divine judgement.

Paul returns to this latter sense of 'clothed' in 5:4, but introduces a new complication by mentioning 'unclothed'. The immediate temptation is to take this as equivalent to 'naked' in the previous verse, but this would make nonsense of his meaning. The parenthetical character of 5:3 should not be lost sight of. Paul's point is the very natural one that he would prefer not to have to undergo the experience of death; he longs to be transported to heaven ('to be further clothed') to enjoy the immortality of eschatological life. It is clear from 1 Corinthians 15:51–4, written only a year earlier, that he expected to be alive at the *Parousia* (1 Thess. 4:15–17). His recent frightening experience (1:8–9) may have raised some doubts, but they did not weigh against his conviction that the return of Christ was imminent. Events proved him wrong, but the influence of this expectation on his theology should not be underestimated.

If the constitution of the person is adapted to life in this world, and if the world to come is radically different, then the constitution of the person must be adapted for survival in a new environment. Paul recognizes the need for such change in 1 Corinthians 15:51–4, and here he gives us a hint of how he expected it to come about (5:5). God has prepared us for eschatological life by giving us 'the down-payment of the Spirit'. The Spirit is the basis of 'life' in the existential sense. It is the power of the gospel (1 Cor. 2:4; 1 Thess. 1:5), which enables a mode of being animated by love. That Spirit, however, is not given in its fullness; it is only an earnest of something more to come: at the *Parousia* it will transform believers completely. Given such a guarantee, it is natural that Paul should proclaim himself as always being of good cheer (5:6a).

But then he suddenly has a most disagreeable surprise. He realizes that what he has just said (4:16–5:5) could be mis-interpreted. In order to justify his confidence in the future, he had spoken of the present in such a way as to appear to devalue bodily existence. He had dismissed the visible realities of the present as transitory and valueless compared with the eternal and invisible (4:18). In particular, his disparaging symbol for present existence, 'tent-like house', could easily be understood as a reference to the body by the Spirit-people since Philo had defined the body as a 'tent' (*Quaestiones in Genesin*, 1:28; cf. Wis. 9:15). This was a serious matter, because he had already had to argue against the slogan of the Spirit-people 'every sin which a person may commit is outside the body' (1 Cor. 6:18), which meant that the body was morally irrelevant. Since no corporeal action had any ultimate significance, everything was permissible (1 Cor. 6:12; 10:23). Paul, on the contrary, believed that commitment to God in Christ became real only in and through the body when love was expressed in actions. This was fundamental to his theology and to his pastoral strategy, and he could not risk appearing to back down from the strong position he had taken in 1 Corinthians.

In order to bring the matter into the open, Paul cites a phrase that expresses the misunderstanding of his opponents: 'being at home in the body we are in exile from the Lord' (5:6b).[39] To be at home in the body is to regard it as one's true dwelling place. For Philo this was the antithesis of true virtue and implied alienation from God: 'You must change your abode and betake yourself to your father's land . . . and that land is Wisdom' (*De Migratione*, 28; cf. *De Somniis*, 1:181); 'The celestial and heavenly soul . . . has left the region of earth, has been drawn upwards, and dwells with divine natures' (*Deus*, 151). Given this perspective, the Spirit-people could claim that they walked 'by faith and not by sight' (5:7).

Paul's response is commonly assumed to mean that he has decided to go to heaven rather than remain on earth (5:8), but this cannot be correct. In Philippians, which cannot be very distant in time from the writing of 2 Corinthians 1–9, Paul makes it perfectly clear that while his *desire* is 'to depart and be with Christ' (1:19), his *decision* is that 'to remain in the flesh is more necessary on your account . . . for your progress and joy in the faith' (1:24–5). If he still had work to do at Philippi, he

---

[39] Only this hypothesis adequately accounts for all the features of this verse, which is usually interpreted as if 'to be at home in the body' were 'to walk according to the flesh'; see my '"Being at home in the body we are in exile from the Lord" (2 Cor. 5:6b)', *RB* 93 (1986), 214–21.

had much more to accomplish at Corinth, and was looking forward to new mission fields (2 Cor. 10:16). It would be a complete misunderstanding of Letter A to imagine that opposition at Corinth had made Paul want to give up completely. Letter B proves exactly the opposite.

None of these difficulties arise if we assume that the choice is between the view of reality expressed in the Corinthians' slogan (5:6b) and that which Paul is about to formulate. In the slogan we are invited to agree that 'in the flesh' means 'away from the Lord'. This static dichotomy Paul cannot accept, so he modifies the slogan by switching the verbs and substituting 'from' for 'in' and 'to' for 'away from' (5:8). This has the effect of introducing the idea of motion, which links the two states. Instead of a chasm between the present and the eschaton there is a difference only of degree. Existential 'life' is a movement towards eschatological 'life'.

Paul retains the verbs of the slogan in 5:8, but while 'to go away from home' is adapted to the idea of motion, 'to be at home' is not. Thus it is not really surprising that he abandons both verbs in 5:9, where 'either being at home or going away from home' is dismissed as irrelevant. The only thing that matters is that believers should live in such a way as to please the Lord (1 Thess. 4;1), and to underline this Paul highlights the fact that all will have to submit to judgement by God (5:10). In the light of what was happening at Corinth it is very significant that he notes that the basis of the divine judgement is 'what is done in and through the body'. To be a Christian is not a matter of intellect or motive but to live aflame with love (1 Cor. 13).

RECONCILIATION IN A NEW CREATION (5:11–6:10)

Paul's evocation of the basis of the final judgement brings his mind back to the present, and the situation at Corinth comes more clearly into focus than at any time since 4:1–6. A correct understanding of his ministry is still his major concern, but he articulates it in such a way that it becomes a paradigm for comportment of all Christians.

It is surprising to find Paul saying 'we persuade men' (5:11), because he had already refused to operate by means of 'persuasive words of wisdom' (1 Cor. 2:4; cf. Gal. 1:10). The only explanation is that this was part of his new strategy for dealing with the Spirit-people. They had accused him of lacking oratorical gifts (4:3), and he here appropriates their term in order to show them what true 'persuasiveness' really is. In opposition to his adversaries, who refused to give Christ his rightful role (4:2), Paul does not practise any deception because he operates under the threat of judgement (4:10) and the fear it inspires (4:11a). He is totally open before God. Can they say as much?

In speaking thus, Paul is in fact recommending himself (5:12a), and his sensitivity to the type of accusation that might be levelled against him in consequence is clear from 3:1. It seems likely that he takes the risk here because the Judaizers were indulging in self-recommendation of the most blatant kind. Their advertising of their visions and revelations (12:1) and their miracles (12:12) was the key to their persuasive effect among the Corinthians. Paul attempts to nullify this approach by giving his converts the sort of data which would enable them to respond to those who judge a person by his appearance rather than by his character (4:12b). The whole of this section (2:14–6:10) furnishes just such data on Paul's ministry, but he now brings it into tight focus.

He deflates the importance of visions and revelations by a simple but very pointed observation (5:13). If he has ever been swept up into ecstasy it is a matter between himself and God, and basically irrelevant because his ministry is concerned with humanity, not with God. In ecstasy one is closed off from the world. Only those who are fully in control of themselves can be at the service of the community. Ministry consists not in self-gratification but total dedication to the well-being of others, as exemplified in the life of Christ. The love shown by Christ is the decisive influence on Paul's life (5:14a). His example is so compelling that he feels that he has been laid hold of by Jesus (Phil. 3:12). Necessity has been laid upon him and he cannot be or do otherwise (1 Cor. 9:16) than exhibit 'the life of Jesus' (4:10–11).

The totality of Jesus' commitment is highlighted by the stark phrase 'one died for all' (5:14b). His concern encompassed all humanity and he gave himself completely. The apparently innocuous words 'for all' has been the key element in a whole plethora of theories of redemption. The clearest indication that Paul did not intend to explain exactly how the death of Christ benefited others is the fact that he uses different prepositions interchangeably. To search for nuances is pointless; all that can be gleaned from a representative series of statements (1 Thess. 5:10; 1 Cor. 15:3; Gal. 2:20; Rom. 5:8; 14:15) is that the death of Christ was in the interest of humanity. Only such a generic expression accurately reflects the state of Christian soteriology in the middle of the first century AD.

Paul's own interpretation of the traditional formula is 'therefore all died' (5:14c). This is designed to shock the Corinthians, who probably expected the opposite, i.e. 'in Christ all shall be made alive' (1 Cor. 15:22). Which of these senses of 'death' is appropriate here (cf. p. 31 above)? No one died physically simply because Christ did; neither did anyone suffer eschatological condemnation. In the existential sense 'death' is a mode of being opposed to God's design for humanity. Those who were hostile to God were not made so by Christ's death. Hence, the only possible meaning is that they were *seen* to be 'dead'![40] They thought of their egocentric existence as normal. The altruism of Christ's existence culminating in his self-sacrifice shattered that illusion. The purpose of Christ's death is to reveal that those who are only physically alive, because they make themselves the centre of their little world, should become existentially alive by dedicating themselves to Christ, who gave his all for them, and through him to all those who need to be raised from 'death' to 'life' (5:15).

This interpretation of 5:14–15, in which the death of Christ

---

[40] Plummer writes: 'they all died in Him in the sense that his supreme act of love extinguished in them the old life of worldly interests in which the centre of gravity was self' (*2 Corinthians*, 174). Even a superficial inspection of the real world reveals this to be untrue. This type of interpretation is redeemed somewhat by Barrett's adverb, 'all men became potentially dead in the sense about to be described in the next verse' (*2 Corinthians*, 168). Ultimately, however, it fails to do justice to the past tense.

appears as the fundamental criterion of human existence, is confirmed by what follows, where Paul confronts the basic issue of Christian epistemology.[41]

The assertion that Paul once knew Christ *kata sarka*, 'according to the flesh', has sparked off a great controversy, because if *kata sarka* is understood as an adjective qualifying 'Christ' it means that Paul had encountered Christ during his earthly ministry. An extreme version of this interpretation makes Paul the rich young man who refused Jesus' invitation to become a disciple (Matt. 19:16–22).[42] In itself an encounter between Paul and Jesus is not impossible, because he was certainly living in Jerusalem when Jesus came on pilgrimage during his ministry. This line of interpretation, however, is excluded by the fact that when Paul uses *kata sarka* as an adjective it follows the noun (cf. 1 Cor. 1:26; 10:18; Rom. 4:1; 9:3). Here it precedes the noun, and so it must be understood as an adverb qualifying 'to know'. When he says 'We once knew Christ in a fleshly way' (5:16b) he is obviously referring to the knowledge he had of Christ when as a Pharisee he persecuted Christians (Gal. 1:13; Phil. 3:6). He shared the view common among his contemporaries that Jesus was an heretical teacher and a turbulent agitator whose activities had rightly brought him to the scaffold. This, he now knows, was a false assessment, and he has abandoned it. He now recognizes Jesus as the Saviour.

This unusual glimpse into Paul's inner life is used to strengthen an implicit appeal to the Corinthians (5:16a), which he presents as the conclusion to be drawn from 5:14–15. It is typical of Paul that he should express it in terms of his own behaviour. A precise parallel is furnished by 1 Corinthians 8:13. At the end of a discussion concerning the principles governing the legitimacy of eating meat offered to idols, he

---

[41] See in particular J. W. Fraser, 'Paul's Knowledge of Jesus: 2 Cor 5:16 Once Again', *NTS* 17 (1970–1), 293–313, and J. L. Martyn, 'Epistemology at the Turn of the Ages: 2 Cor 5:16', in W. Farmer, C. Moule and R. R. Niebuhr (eds.), *Christian History and Interpretation (Festschrift* for J. Knox; Cambridge, 1967), 269–87.

[42] A. M. Pope, 'Paul's Previous Meeting with Jesus', *Expositor* 26 (1923), 38–48.

refuses to tell the Corinthians what to do. Instead he tells them what he would do in the same circumstances.[43]

'We know no one in a fleshly way' (5:16a) implies that others do. Paul is thinking of those who assessed his performance as a minister by the standards applied to pagan orators. They should have judged him as a follower of Christ. The underlying principle, however, has a much wider application. The Corinthians had entered the church as adult converts, and inevitably brought with them a way of looking at humanity which they had assimilated from a world dominated by Sin. They took for granted certain patterns of behaviour simply because they were widespread: for example, jealousy, strife and party factions were a feature of social life as they knew it. In consequence, they were in no way disconcerted when these developed within the church; that was the way life was. In response, Paul claimed that they were 'fleshly' and 'walking according to man' (1 Cor. 3:1–14). In his lexicon 'according to man' means a judgement based on the common estimation of a sinful world (1 Cor. 9:8; 15:32; Gal. 3:15; Rom. 3:5; contrast 'according to God', 2 Cor. 7:9–10). Their standard was what everybody does, whereas their criterion should have been Christ, whose death revealed creative unifying love as the distinctive possibility which defines human nature (5:15). Having encountered Christ through Paul's preaching and in the sacraments of baptism and eucharist, they should have said 'We know no one in a fleshly way' and developed a pattern of community life governed by an authentic vision of what humanity was capable of when freed from Sin.

It should be emphasized that Paul's perspective here is the reverse of that adopted by many modern theologians. Their starting point is that 'Christ is a man like us' and they attempt to develop an understanding of the humanity of Christ by extrapolating from the observed characteristics of contemporary humanity.[44] Thus they say that Christ suffered doubt and

---

[43] Georgi's hypothesis that in 5:16–17 Paul is dealing with the Christology of his opponents (*Opponents of Paul*, 252–3 and 276–7) is singularly unconvincing.

[44] See, for example, J. Knox, *The Humanity and Divinity of Christ* (Cambridge, 1967), 63–8; or P. de Rosa, *Christ and Original Sin* (London, 1967), 43.

fear, that he had to struggle to discern his vocation and to remain faithful to it. They do not say, however, that he was greedy or possessive, and their method furnishes no basis for such discrimination. Paul, on the contrary, realized that the observable characteristics are those of *fallen* humanity and can never yield a portrait of humanity *as such*. Thus he insists that we must first know the humanity of Christ if we are to discern what is good and bad in human nature, because as the New Adam he reveals what authentic humanity is.[45]

Paul is so conscious of the radical nature of the shift in perspective which this involves that he claims that 'anyone who is in Christ is a new creature' (5:17a). Since he predicates Christ of the believing community (1 Cor. 6:15; 12:12), to be 'in Christ' is simply to belong to the church. Those who once were 'dead' are now 'alive' because they belong to Christ (1 Cor. 3:23). For them, all has changed in such a fundamental sense that each is now a 'new creature'.[46] How has this come about? 'The old things', i.e. the criteria which governed their behaviour in the world, have passed away. In their place are 'the new things': namely, the new standards of judgement revealed in the humanity of Christ (5:17b).

This stress on a renewed judgement (Col. 3:11) as the basis of a pattern of behaviour different from that of the world is demanded by the context. But what about baptism? Baptism for Paul is essentially a rite of initiation into an alternative environment – the Christian community (Gal. 3:26–8). It is not a magical gesture which transforms the individual automatically. Moving from enslavement to Sin (Rom. 6:17) into freedom, believers enter a community of opportunity where authentic values reign. As they assimilate the lesson of the

---

[45] On this fundamental Pauline theme see C. K. Barrett, *From First Adam to Last. A Study in Pauline Theology* (London, 1962); R. Scroggs, *The Last Adam. A Study in Pauline Anthropology* (Philadelphia, 1966).

[46] Barrett translates 'if anyone is in Christ there is a new act of creation', but understands it vaguely as the inauguration of the new age (*2 Corinthians*, 173). If the object of the new act of creation is the one who is in Christ then that person is a new creature. Note in particular Col. 3:10–11, where knowledge and newness of being are combined as here. For Furnish the 'new creation' is cosmic in scope (*II Corinthians*, 333), but it is difficult to see how he can justify the logic implicit in his interpretation; if one individual is changed, then the cosmos has been changed!

death of Christ (5:15) they are progressively transformed
(3:18). This process had broken down at Corinth. The inauthentic values of the world continued to exercise a decisive
influence on the behaviour of the community. This had a
detrimental effect on the quality of life, and incidentally led to
Paul being judged in worldly terms. Thus, both pastorally and
personally, he had to insist on the fundamental truth: Christ is
the criterion.

Having dealt with salvation subjectively (5:14–18), i.e. how
human beings appropriate the saving event of Christ's death,
Paul now treats the same topic objectively using a traditional
formulation (5:19a, b).[47] His choice of this element of tradition
was probably motivated by the fact that it mentions reconciliation. While perfectly apt to describe the process of salvation, it had an added advantage for Paul, who, it must be
remembered, is writing a letter of reconciliation.

As a convinced monotheist Paul naturally ascribed the
initiative to God. He is the ultimate cause of our salvation; the
agent he chose to put his plan into effect is Christ; 'through
Christ' (5:18) clarifies the possibly ambiguous 'in Christ'
(5:19). How did God use him? 'Him who knew not sin he made
sin on our behalf' (5:21).[48] The sinlessness of Christ is the
common teaching of New Testament writers (John 8:46;
1 John 3:5; Heb. 4:15; 1 Peter 2:22) and derives from their
recognition of him as the Messiah, who, as the Righteous One
(1 Enoch 38:2), would be 'pure from sin' (Ps. of Solomon 17:41;
cf. Test. Judah 24:1; Test. Levi 18:1). As such, he had a right to
immortality, because in Jewish tradition death was not part of
God's original plan for humanity. Interpreting Genesis 1–3,
the sage says 'God did not make death and he does not delight
in the death of the living' (Wis. 1:12), and a little later, 'God
created man in a state of incorruptibility; in the image of his
own eternity he made him, but through the devil's envy death
entered the world' (Wis. 2:23–4). Death came into being as
punishment for sin: 'You laid on Adam one commandment of

---

[47] For documentation of this widespread opinion, see Furnish, *II Corinthians*, 334.
[48] There is a good survey of the history of interpretation in S. Lyonnet and
L. Sabourin, *Sin, Redemption and Sacrifice* (AnBib 48; Rome, 1970), 187–296.

yours but he transgressed it, and immediately you appointed death for him and for his descendants' (4 Ezra 3:7; cf. 2 Baruch. 23:4). None the less Christ suffered and died, even though he was not a sinner. In other words, he was subject to the consequences of sin. Only in this sense is the extraordinary phrase 'he made him sin' intelligible. Christ entered into the human situation so totally that he accepted the lot of all members of a fallen humanity.

Did Christ's death in itself have the effect of reconciling humanity with God? Obviously not; otherwise Paul's ministry would be pointless. His appeal underlines the need for human response and co-operation (6:1). This means, of course, that his statement, 'God reconciled us to himself' (5:18), cannot be taken literally, even if we add 'not counting their trespasses against them' (5:19). If taken at face value this would mean that God decided to ignore the sins of humanity; from an attitude of wrath he simply switched to one of benevolence. Thus it is God who changes, not humanity, giving the impression that humanity was in the right and that it was up to God to make concessions. This ridiculous conclusion cannot be what Paul intended to say. His stress on the act of faith elsewhere (Gal. 3:26–7; Rom. 10:9–10) shows that in his haste here he has left out a series of steps that are essential to the salvific process. If God is to respect the free decision-making nature that he gave his creatures, he cannot make them righteous. All that he can do is to make it possible for them effectively to choose righteousness, i.e. to conform themselves to his intention for humanity (5:21). Only when they exist as God intended them to be are they reconciled with God. God's forgiveness reaches out to them, but in their turn they have to renounce sin.

Within history Christ appeared as 'the wisdom and power of God' (1 Cor. 1:24). He revealed in his person and comportment the divine intention for humanity, and a power (grace) radiated from him, which broke the power of Sin that held humanity enslaved (Rom. 3:9). Thus those who encountered him during his earthly ministry were both given a vision of the ideal and enabled to follow it. These, however, were very few by comparison with the mass of humanity. Were others to be excluded from salvation simply because they lived in the wrong place or were born at the wrong time? Paul answers in the negative. God made provision for the post-resurrection period by appointing him (and others) to carry on the work of Christ. The ministry of Christ, as we have just seen, had two dimensions: the existential and the verbal. Both have to be maintained if reconciliation is to remain a real possibility. The existential aspect is conserved in so far as Paul manifests 'the life of Jesus' (4:10–11). Here, therefore, he highlights the verbal aspects, 'We are ambassadors on behalf of Christ, God appealing through us' (5:20). As God once acted in and through Christ, so now he acts in and through Paul to demonstrate and proclaim. Thus Paul is 'God's co-worker' (6:1; cf. 1 Cor. 3:9; 1 Thess. 3:2), the supreme title accorded to an apostle. God could have decided to act in other ways, but in fact he chose to extend his invitation to reconciliation through human agents. Those who respond opt to be conformed to Christ (Rom. 8:29) and are thereby reconciled with God.

The Corinthians had accepted Christ intellectually, but their behaviour indicated that they were not yet conformed to Christ. The various forms of egocentricity they displayed contrasted radically with the altruism of Christ. They had received the grace of God, but there was a real danger that it would remain without meaningful effect (6:1). Paul, in consequence, has to appeal for their reconversion (6:2b). He reinforces his appeal with a citation from Isaiah 49:8 (6:2a), whose meaning is totally transformed by the context. The Jewish author looked forward to 'the day of salvation'. Since, for Paul, the Messiah had come, every day was the day of salvation; grace was always available, and it was never too late to respond.

In the new dispensation, however, grace is mediated through human channels, and Paul was conscious that his inadequacy could block the transmission of grace which enabled the Corinthians to respond to God's invitation: he could rob the cross of Christ of its power (1 Cor. 1:17); his ministry could be a stumbling block (6:3). Such is the awesome responsibility of ministers! Thus he is led to insist that in his ministry grace is available to the Corinthians (6:3). He does so in a catalogue whose lyrical language and rhetorical structure create a fitting conclusion to this long section on ministry.

The first nine items on the list (6:4c–5) illustrate his endurance. Perseverance in the face of difficulties is the most easily recognizable sign of complete dedication. Egocentricities fade into the background when their self-interest is no longer gratified. 'Afflictions, hardships, calamities' are very generic, but he immediately goes on to illustrate what he means by examples taken from the way he is ill used by others ('beatings, imprisonments, riots') and from the difficulties he has in paying his way ('labours, sleepless nights, hunger'). He made it a principle not to take money from any community in which he was working (1 Cor. 9:12–18), but supported himself as he travelled and preached. Since a stable artisan with a regular clientele and who worked full time at this trade barely made ends meet in the first century, this meant that Paul had a very rough time. But to exact payment would limit the appeal of his gospel and thus compromise the generosity of God's invitation.

Having established the framework within which he lived his ministry, Paul then describes its characteristics (6:6–7a). His detachment guarantees his 'purity' of motive. In dealing with the Corinthians he had shown 'knowledge, forbearance and kindness', although in differing degrees to various sections of the community. Some translations and commentators capitalize 'Holy Spirit', but it is more likely that Paul intends to evoke the holiness of spirit that should characterize redeemed humanity (1 Thess. 4:3–7). His 'genuine love' for the Corinthians expressed itself in 'truthful speech'. His concern for their salvation would not permit him to hide behind illusions, and even at the risk of alienating them he said what had to be said. Others, such as the Judaizers, pandered to the expectations of a section of the community. A ministry informed by insight, practical concern and honesty is a perfect channel for 'the power of God'.

The next literary unit in the catalogue (6:7b–8a) is the most difficult to characterize. It serves as a transition to the last element. The mention of 'power' brought to mind the associated idea of 'weapons'. Paul is armed with 'righteousness' both in attack (the sword or spear was carried in the right hand) and defence (the shield was slung on the left arm). In attack he could be 'renowned' and 'praised'. The Galatians, for example, had received Paul 'as an angel of God, as Jesus Christ' (Gal. 4:14); but he could also suffer defeat and be 'dishonoured' and 'defamed', as he had been at Corinth.

This contrast prepares the way for the seven antitheses which conclude the catalogue (6:8b–10). In each pair the first term reflects the way Paul has been perceived by those who judge according to the standards of the world, whereas the second mirrors his own vision of himself, which he trusts will be shared by all who have accepted Christ as their criterion. Rhetorical passion often leads to exaggeration, but Paul's claims amount to no more than a modest confirmation of his assertion that he embodies 'the life of Jesus' (4:10–11), 'who for your sake became poor, so that by his poverty you might become rich' (8:9).

CHAPTER 5

Relations with Corinth (6:11–7:16)

The direct address, 'Corinthians' (6:11), indicates the beginning of a new section of Letter A. All that Paul said in the long section on ministry (2:14–6:10) was, despite its wider applications, directly relevant to the situation at Corinth, but the allusions to precise issues occurred only in the form of delicate hints and subtle allusions. Such issues concerned the attempts of the Spirit-people and the Judaizers to undermine his position. The Judaizers who had come from outside were Paul's concern only to the extent that they were disrupting his community. Even though he had changed his mind after the episode at Antioch (Gal. 2:11–21), he had officially accepted their vision of Christianity as valid for believers of Jewish stock (Gal. 2:9), and was not prepared, on this occasion at least, to argue them out of their position. He believed that he had said enough (3:7–18) to destroy their influence at Corinth, and so he now turns his attention to the community.

Even though Titus had brought word (7:6–7) that the community had been reconciled with Paul, this referred to the church as a whole, and Paul still had some doubt about the attitude of the Spirit-people. Thus he begins by begging them to respond to the generosity that he has shown (6:11–7:4), and then turns to a further discussion of the incident which had soured his relations with the community and had given rise to the Sorrowful Letter (7:5–16; cf. 2:1–11).

AN APPEAL FOR OPENNESS (6:11–7:4)

In order to explain the rather abrupt transition from 6:10, a
number of associative links have to be postulated. The words
'possessing everything' brought to Paul's mind a fundamental
Old Testament theme: great material rewards were promised
to those who obeyed the commandment 'to love the Lord your
God, and to serve him with your whole heart and with your
whole soul' (Deut. 11:13–15). Associated with this, however,
was a warning: 'But when you have eaten and are full, take
heed that your heart does not grow wide, and that you do not
transgress and serve other gods and worship them' (Deut.
11:16). The idea of a 'wide heart' recalled to Paul the fact that
the hearts of the Spirit-people were not fully open to him; he
was not sure to what extent they shared in the reconciliatory
attitude of the community. Thus this aspect moved to the front
of his mind.

Paul has spoken to them in complete freedom, and assures
them that there is room for them in his heart (6:11). They
cannot claim that he has excluded them; if there is any
restriction in their emotional relationship it is on their side
(6:12). Therefore, they should respond in kind (6:13b). Despite
his rather brutal treatment of them in 1 Corinthians, Paul may
honestly have believed this to be the case; but he cannot forget
that they had been the strongest critics of his leadership, and
this aspect immediately surfaces. 'I speak as to children'
(6:13a) is ambiguous. At first sight it appears to betray Paul's
paternal affection, as in 1 Corinthians 4:14, and Galatians
4:19. In both of these texts, however, the possessive pronoun
'my' qualifies 'children' and the theme of spiritual paternity is
explicit. No such affective connotation is visible here. In fact,
the formulation is reminiscent only of 1 Corinthians 3:1: 'I
could not address you as Spirit-people, but as fleshly, as
children in Christ.' This was a sharp put-down to those who
prided themselves on their spiritual perfection, because Philo
had said, 'We see clearly that he has given the name of
"children" to those within whose souls are grounds for blame,
who so often fall through folly and senselessness, and fail to do

what the upright life requires' (*De Sobrietate*, 11). Paul's cool tone suggests the same meaning here (6:13a), and this is born out by what follows.

For many scholars 6:14–7:1 is non-Pauline:[49] some assert that Paul is here citing material which he did not write himself; while others maintain that it was inserted into Letter A by the editor who combined this letter with Letter B to create the present 2 Corinthians. Both groups, however, claim that it cannot have been written by Paul, because it contains a series of words which are not used elsewhere in the epistles, and because it exhibits a high concentration of Essene parallels found in the Dead Sea Scrolls.

The first argument carries no weight. Other passages of Paul's letters contain even higher percentages of once-used words. The Essene parallels lose much of their significance once it is realized that a more complete set of parallels can be found in the works of Philo. There is no need, therefore, to postulate Essene derivation. The ideas were available in the Hellenistic-Jewish world. In view of the influence of Philo on the Spirit-people, it appears likely that Paul is adapting Philonic concepts, which he could have learnt from Apollos (1 Cor. 16:12), in order to reorientate the thinking of the Spirit-people.

Paul begins with an imperative (6:14a) in which he invokes the Jewish prohibition against unnatural combinations (Lev. 19:19; Deut. 22:9–11), and the function of the rhetorical questions which follow (6:14b–16a) is to insinuate the scope of the imperative. The fourth antithesis (6:15b) indicates that Paul considers 'belief' and 'unbelief' an unnatural combination. It simply articulates in another form the initial imperative which, of course, is addressed to believers. This repetition highlights 'belief–unbelief' as the fundamental issue. At first sight, it would seem that Paul is insisting that Christians should not associate with Jews or pagans; but this is excluded by his general attitude towards mission, and by the fact that he

---

[49] Furnish offers a comprehensive survey of opinions (*II Corinthians*, 375–83). I am convinced that Paul wrote this passage for this place in the letter; see my 'Philo and 2 Cor. 6:14–7:1', *RB* 95 (1988), 55–69.

has no objection to Christians eating with unbelievers (1 Cor. 10:27). The way out of this impasse is furnished by Philo, for whom 'unbelief' is less a negative attitude (lack of faith) than a positive commitment to transitory, created things: 'belief in those things is disbelief in God, and disbelief in them belief in God' (*De Abrahamo*, 269). What Paul wants to dissociate is belief in God revealed by Christ and a commitment to earthly, transitory realities.

Yet this unnatural combination was precisely what the Spirit-people manifested. They were Christians, but none the less they were slaves to the conventions of their age in so far as they judged Paul according to the standards of the world (4:3–4) because they stressed the visible and transient (4:18; 5:12). They demonstrated a combination of belief and unbelief which Matthew would have called 'little faith' (6:30; 8:26; 14:31; 16:8). Thus one might paraphrase the imperative 'Do not blend belief and unbelief' (6:14a).

This interpretation implies that 'iniquity' (6:14b), 'darkness' (6:14c), 'Belial' (6:15a) and 'idols' (6:16a) are to be associated with the Spirit-people. Any idea that this might be an objection is dispelled by 1 Corinthians. The clearest instance of 'iniquity' at Corinth is the case of incest (1 Cor. 5:1–5), which was condemned by both Jews and Gentiles. Since they considered all corporeal activity morally neutral (1 Cor. 6:18b), it is very probable that the Spirit-people were among those who approved of it (1 Cor. 5:2). Equally, they are to be identified with the Strong, who, by sitting at table in an idol's temple (1 Cor. 8:10), became partners with demons (1 Cor. 10:20), and so did the work of Belial by destroying the Weak, for whom Christ died (1 Cor. 8:11).

Paul invites them to move from such 'darkness' to the 'light' of Christ (4:3–4). His appeal to the sanctity of God's temple (6:16), which the series of Old Testament citations is designed to support, is an argument that he has already used, and precisely in a context concerning the Spirit-people (1 Cor. 6:19). The identification of the community as a spiritual temple also appears at Qumran (*IQS*, 8:5–9) but it is unlikely that Paul borrowed the idea from the Essenes because the components of the two concepts are different. The Essenes derived it from the idea of prayer as a spiritual sacrifice (*IQS*, 9:3–5), whereas Paul derived it from the presence of the Holy Spirit in the community (1 Cor. 3:16–17). This imposed an obligation on all members to cleanse themselves 'from every fleshly and spiritual defilement' (7:1) and to become perfect in holiness.

The theme of the spiritual temple having directed Paul's attention to the whole community, he repeats his invitation (6:13b); 'Open your hearts to us' (7:2a). He deserves such a response because, unlike the Spirit-people whose 'corrupting' influence on the community is manifest throughout 1 Corinthians, he never 'wronged' anyone (2:1–13), nor did he 'defraud' them either intellectually (2:17; 4:2) or financially (11:19–20). Whatever he might have suffered at their hands, he has nothing but love for them in his heart. To express the depth of his affection he uses the classical formula for abiding friendship and loyalty 'to live together and to die together' (cf. 2 Sam. 15:21), but typically adapts it by inverting the order (7:3b) so that it becomes a subtle invitation to die to Sin and to live for Christ (5:15).

THE RESULTS OF THE MISSION OF TITUS (7:5–16)

The mention of divine 'comfort' (7:4) recalls to Paul's mind the outstanding recent example of God's benevolence in his regard, the good news brought by Titus of the effect which the Sorrowful Letter (2:4) had had at Corinth.[50] He had touched on the matter already (2:5–11) in discussing the action taken by the community with regard to the one responsible for the incident, and some scholars have thought that this section was originally the direct continuation of 2:13. Such a connection is both grammatically awkward (2:13 is singular and 7:5 is plural) and psychologically implausible, since the aspect treated here, the repentance of the community, must have been prior to the punishment inflicted on the culprit.

The 'fear' which Paul experienced in Macedonia must have

50 For the background to this episode see the reference on p. 25 note 20 above.

been caused by anxiety regarding the reception the Sorrowful Letter would receive at Corinth. If he had miscalculated in writing as he did, his relationship with the community might have come to an end. In the light of his correspondence with Philippi and Thessalonica, it is unlikely that 'disputes' (7:5) refers to problems within these churches. Both were objects of persecution (8:2; cf. Phil. 1:27–30; 1 Thess. 2:14) and he must have become embroiled in rather nasty incidents. But just when he was in very bad shape, both psychically and physically, God acted to strengthen him (cf. 1:3–6). There was no mysterious infusion of grace which transformed his depression into euphoria, but the providential arrival of a friend with good news (7:6–7). As always, God acted through human channels.

It is very human of Paul to regret a harsh letter once it had produced the desired effect (7:8), and his fumbling language betrays his concern not to undo the good that had been achieved by an expression susceptible of misinterpretation (cf. 1:13). The letter had two effects, one temporary the other lasting. It produced grief, which was hurtful to the Corinthians, and it produced repentance, which was beneficial to them. The two are necessarily related, and Paul had to make it clear that he rejoiced in the latter but not in the former. It would have been potentially disastrous to give the impression that he had taken pleasure in the suffering of the Corinthians. With a prolixity born of embarrassment, he distinguishes between 'worldly grief' and 'godly grief' (7:10). The former is the feeling of shame at the injury done to the other. It breeds self-destructive resentment, which is why Paul describes its consequence as existential 'death'. 'Godly grief', on the other hand, turns outward and is other-directed. It is regret for what has happened and embodies a willingness to repair the damage.

The health of the Corinthians' grief was evidenced by its fruits. Their repentance, which showed that they were back on the way of salvation (7:10), found practical expression in a series of attitudes (7:11). They were 'earnest' about the matter. They saw that it was not something which could be shrugged

off as if it were a matter of no consequence. They had furnished
a convincing 'defence' of their position in the affair. Most
likely, they showed that they had not instigated the insult to
Paul. Their 'indignation' was directed at the intruder who had
abused their hospitality. They had become 'alarmed' at the
possibility of losing Paul's respect and friendship, and 'longed'
to see him again. In their 'eagerness' they were ready to do
anything to please him, and had taken 'vengeance' on the
culprit. From Paul's perspective the slate had been wiped
clean, and they could begin anew a relationship strengthened
by shared suffering (7:11b).

Were Paul a self-centred person his vindication by such a
reaction on the part of the Corinthians would have been
uppermost in his mind. The extent to which he in fact
embodied 'the life of Jesus' (4:10–11) is manifest in that his
primary focus was the fate of the one who had offended him.
When he first touched on this sorry episode (2:5–11) he was
extremely concerned that the punishment inflicted on him
might be too harsh and therefore counterproductive. Love was
integral to his being (1 Cor. 13:2) and the driving force of his
ministry (5:14).

Punishment of the one responsible was not Paul's purpose in
writing the Sorrowful Letter (2:4), nor was his own vindication
(6:12). His sole concern was the attitude of the community.
Their neutrality worried him seriously because it indicated a
lack of the love that should be the hallmark of Christians.
Whatever the rights and wrongs of the affair they had made no
effort to compose the quarrel. They had not tried to reconcile
the disputants. Had they attempted to assist, they might have
functioned as the channel of grace which would have permitted
Paul and his opponent to rise above their differences and find
common ground in Christ. Paul found their failure so upsetting
because it indicated a basic flaw in their understanding of what
it meant to be a Christian. They had not adequately realized
that they had to reach out to one another.

In response to the Sorrowful Letter, however, they had
reached out to Paul (7:11) and he was sure that they would also
do so to the offender (2:8). Their true selves in the sight of God

had been revealed to them. They had manifested in practice what it meant to be Christians, and Paul was 'comforted' (7:13a). Again he had seen grace at work. His letter had been used by God to promote the spiritual development of the Corinthians.

The letter, however, had been conveyed by Titus and it was he who brought the longed-for response (7:13b).[51] He is not mentioned in Acts, but appears as one of Paul's companions at the Jerusalem conference (Gal. 2:1). All that is known of him is that he was a gentile (Gal. 2:3). He was probably selected for this delicate mission, because Timothy, Paul's preferred emissary, had run into trouble at Corinth (1 Cor. 4:17; 16:10–11), which provoked the visit when Paul himself had been insulted (2:1). Titus must have been extremely apprehensive at the responsibility entrusted to him. If Paul and Timothy had failed, what could be achieve? He was carrying, furthermore, a potentially explosive letter! Naturally, he was delighted to have his mind set at rest by the warm reception he got at Corinth (7:13b). Subsequent events, as reflected in Letter B (2 Cor. 10–13), indicate that Titus' sense of relief probably led him to give somewhat too optimistic a report on the condition of the community (7:15). It is equally possible, of course, that Paul's willingness to catch at straws caused him to read too much into what his agent reported. He badly wanted to believe that all was well.

The rosy haze enveloping Paul's mind affected even his own recollection of his attitude six months earlier, when he wrote the Sorrowful Letter and dispatched Titus (7:14). If he wrote 'out of much affliction and anguish of heart and with many tears' (2:4), and if he was so uncertain about the result (2:13; 7:5), it seems highly unlikely that he could have painted the Corinthians in the positive light that 7:14 implies. In order to boost Titus' confidence, he would have had to say something good about them, but this can hardly have been more than a generic statement that they were basically sincere. The results, however, exceeded his expectations, and the euphoria led him

---

[51] See C. K. Barrett, 'Titus', in E. E. Ellis and M. Wilcox (eds.), *Neotestamentica et Semitica* (Festschrift for Black; Edinburgh, 1969), 1–14.

to believe that he had thought all along that they were really good, responsible people. In a mood of 'perfect confidence' (7:16), therefore, he makes the appeal for money for Jerusalem in the next two chapters.[52]

[52] There may also be an element of conscious manipulation in such expressions of confidence (7:4, 14), because, as S. N. Olsen has argued, 'The epistolary expression of confidence is best interpreted as a persuasive technique rather than as a sincere reflection of the way the writer thinks the addressees will respond to his proposals or to himself' ('Pauline Expressions of Confidence in his Addressees', *CBQ* 47 (1985), 282–95, here 295). From this perspective chapter 7 lays the groundwork for chapter 8, and constitutes an argument against the hypothesis that chapter 8 was originally an independent letter (cf. note 55).

CHAPTER 6

The collection for Jerusalem (8:1–9:15)

At the Jerusalem conference in the autumn of AD 51 James, Cephas and John accepted the legitimacy of the gospel that Paul preached to the gentiles. They suggested no changes, but they did make a request: namely, that he organize a collection for the financial assistance of 'the poor'. Paul, of course, agreed (Gal. 2:10), and this became one of his principal concerns during his great missionary journey of the years AD 52–6.[53]

Absolutely speaking, 'the poor' could be understood as a religious designation of the members of the community. The theme is well represented in the Old Testament, and the Essenes thought of themselves as 'the congregation of the poor' (4QpPs. 37 2:9–10). This interpretation, however, is excluded by Paul, who elsewhere speaks of the collection as for the benefit of 'the poor among the saints at Jerusalem' (Rom. 15:26). 'The poor' can only be a socio-economic group within the Jerusalem community, who lived a precarious existence on the level of bare subsistence. It has been documented that a large portion of the population of Jerusalem at the time of Jesus lived principally or exclusively on organized relief or individual alms.[54] That a number of Christians belonged to this class is shown by the note in Acts to the effect that wealthy members of the community sold lands and houses in order to subsidize needy members of the church (Acts 2:45; 4:34–5).

---

[53] The two major studies are D. Georgi, *Die Geschichte der Kollekte des Paulus für Jerusalem* (TF 38; Hamburg, 1965), and K. F. Nickle, *The Collection* (SBT 48; London, 1966).

[54] 'Jerusalem had already in Jesus' time become a city of idlers, and ... the considerable proletariat living on the religious importance of the city was one of its most outstanding peculiarities' (J. Jeremias, *Jerusalem in the Time of Jesus. An*

Unless new wealthy members were regularly recruited, this system could have only one end: the community would run out of money. Since it was persecuted by the Jewish authorities (Gal. 1:22–3), there was no hope of aid from traditional sources. That left only the burgeoning gentile church, whose members, though not rich (1 Cor. 1:26; 2 Cor. 8:2), were almost certainly better off than the majority of the Jerusalem community.

In addition to enabling the community to survive, the Jerusalem authorities may have seen a symbolic dimension in this gesture of the gentile churches. Synagogues in the diaspora were obliged to collect a half-shekel tax from each male member and to send it each year to the temple in Jerusalem. The voluntary contributions collected by Paul were in no sense a Christian 'temple tax', but against the background of the Jewish practice the Jerusalem church could have complacently viewed it as recognition of its pre-eminent status as the mother of all churches.

Paul certainly did not see the collection in this light. It was primarily a simple act of charity: those who had a surplus, however small, should share it with those who had nothing as an elementary expression of their Christianity. In speaking of the collection, it is significant that he uses a commercial term, 'contributions', only once (1 Cor. 16:1–2) and then only because he was dealing with an administrative problem. For the most part, as we shall see in these chapters, he uses terms of rich theological significance in order to bring home to the Corinthians that their gesture was integral to their very being as believers. He compares it to the complete self-giving of Christ (8:9).

The collection also had another dimension that was of only slightly lesser significance for Paul. To his dismay, the gentile and Jewish branches of the church were steadily moving further apart, and the relations between the two were often acrimonious, as the Antioch incident shows (Gal. 2:11–21). By the time of the writing of Romans (AD 56) matters had reached

Investigation into Economic and Social Conditions during the New Testament Period (London, 1969), 111–19, here 118).

such a point that he wondered if the collection would be acceptable in Jerusalem (Rom. 15:31). Feelings must have been running very high if there was a danger that badly needed financial assistance would be rejected. None the less he persisted. Authentic love is never motivated by the hope of response, and the only force that could hold the two branches of the church together, despite their differences, was a love which binds everyone together in perfect harmony (Col. 3:14). Each could go its own way, provided that both were truly grounded in 'the love of God in Christ Jesus our Lord' (Rom. 8:39). This, however, had to be more than a theoretical ideal. There had to be some concrete expression, and Paul found it in the collection. There could be many other demonstrations of love, but this one had been requested by Jerusalem, and the need was evident.

On his way from Antioch to Ephesus in the spring of AD 52 Paul preached the collection in Galatia (1 Cor. 16:1). It would have been near the end of the sailing season when he reached Ephesus, and it is unlikely that he could have invited the Corinthians to participate until the following spring. How he did it is unclear, but the simplest hypothesis is that they had heard about it from Chloe's people (1 Cor. 1:11). The Corinthians responded positively, because in their letter to him (1 Cor. 7:1) they only requested his advice as to how the contributions were to be organized.

In order to have a significant sum ready when he arrived, Paul suggested that each member of the community should begin a savings fund to which he or she would add something each Sunday (1 Cor. 16:2). His assumption that all members could contribute tells us something about the economic level of the community: they did not live to the limit of their earnings. Yet the surplus cannot have been very great if each was expected to save in order that the contribution of each might be generous. Paul's common sense is evident in the measures he takes to protect the community and himself. A central fund could give rise to accusations of misappropriation, and if he took charge of the money he might be thought to be motivated by self-interest. Thus the Corinthians themselves are to select those who will bear the collection to Jerusalem (1 Cor. 16:4). This had the added advantage of demonstrating to Jerusalem the success of the gentile mission.

The crisis which developed as a consequence of Paul's visit to Corinth in the early summer of AD 54 meant that this plan was not put into effect. The church's relationship with Paul had been poisoned, and its preoccupation with its own affairs left little room for concern for the needs of the poor in Jerusalem. It is even possible that the Judaizers had minimized the need for the collection in order to diminish Paul's stature.

For the reasons which we have seen, the collection was too important for Paul to let the matter drop. Hence, he capitalizes on the mood of goodwill to raise the issue again. His experience, however, showed him that he should take nothing for granted, and he is concerned not to organize the Corinthians as in 1 Corinthians, but to motivate them. A number of scholars consider these chapters to represent two originally independent letters, one addressed to Corinth (chap. 8) and the other to the province of Achaia (chap. 9), but have failed to present convincing arguments.[55]

A CHALLENGING REQUEST (8:1–15)

After leaving Ephesus for Troas, Paul crossed the sea to Macedonia (2:12–13; 7:5) and spent the winter of AD 54–5 with the communities in Philippi and Thessalonica which were located on the great Roman road, the Via Egnatia, which spanned the breadth of the province. Letter A was certainly written from Macedonia in the spring of AD 55, at a moment when Paul knew the situation of the Macedonian churches

[55] So, rightly, V. P. Furnish, *II Corinthians* (AB; Garden City, NY, 1984), 433. This conclusion has been confirmed rather than infirmed by H. D. Betz, *2 Corinthians 8 and 9. A Commentary on Two Administrative Letters of the Apostle Paul* (Hermeneia; Philadelphia, 1985). The latter's original contribution is to introduce epistolary and rhetorical theory into the debate, but it shows only that these two chapters can be *thought* of as independent letters. All that his analyses *prove*, however, is that when at the end of a letter of reconciliation Paul came to deal with an administrative matter he did so in a business-like way. A number of letters concerned with mission-related finances have been collected by M. Kiely in an appendix to his *Colossians as Pseudepigraphy* (Sheffield, 1986).

intimately. Though no mention of the collection is made in his correspondence with Thessalonica and Philippi, he must have invited them to participate. We do not know how or when he did this, but it must have been prior to the writing of 1 Corinthians, because in the light of 1 Corinthians 16:1–4, the purpose of his planned visit to Macedonia (1 Cor. 16:5), which never came off because of the crisis at Corinth, can only have been to pick up the gift of the Macedonians. The importance of the collection would have been underlined during the visit of Timothy and Erastus (Acts 19:22), and the process would have come to a climax during Paul's sojourn.

What struck Paul most forcibly was the discrepancy between the sum the Macedonians collected and their financial resources. Their 'wealth of generosity' contrasted vividly with their 'rock-bottom poverty' (8:2). Macedonia was not a poor province, and the Via Egnatia was a major east–west trade route, which meant rich pickings for the cities through which it passed. Thus the poverty of Macedonian believers was probably due to 'the severe test of affliction' (8:2). Even though persecution was sporadic (Phil. 1:29; 1 Thess. 2:14; 3:4; Thess. 1:4–10), there was the ongoing harassment that meant loss of jobs and economic opportunities.[56] Under such circumstances their liberality could only be explained as evidence of the 'grace of God' (8:1). The gap between expectation and realization demonstrated the effect of the power of God in their lives. Only a self-sacrificing love modelled on that of Christ (5:15) could have motivated them to give more than they could afford (8:3a).

Even though love is not explicitly mentioned, the concept is certainly in Paul's mind. He did not put any pressure on them, as he is now trying to do to the Corinthians by holding up the example of the Macedonians. His proposal was greeted by spontaneous enthusiasm (8:3b), and they saw the purpose of

[56] R. Jewett has convincingly argued that the Christians of Thessalonica were a classic example of the oppressed poor, victims of the pressures of economics, political powerlessness, and colonial exploitation (*The Thessalonian Correspondence. Pauline Rhetoric and Millenarian Piety* (Philadelphia, 1986), 165–6). Such poverty was exacerbated by the refusal of some members of the community to continue in their normal occupations (1 Thess. 4:11–12; 2 Thess. 3:6–12).

what he was trying to achieve. They saw it not primarily as a financial transaction, but as 'the fellowship of the ministry to the saints' (8:4). The gesture bonded them, not only with the ministry of Christ in Paul, but with the suffering members of another church, whom they had never seen but with whom they shared a common faith. Their response went further than the need. Their generosity was as much, if not more, spiritual as material.

This dimension was of supreme importance to Paul, who abhorred the cold charity which is assistance without involvement. The fundamental gift of the Macedonians was that of themselves (8:5): 'You became imitators of us and of the Lord, for you received the word in much affliction and with joy inspired by the Holy Spirit' (1 Thess. 1:6). Despite dangers which threatened their lives, they had conformed themselves to the self-sacrificing Christ (5:15) by modelling their behaviour on that of Paul who manifested the 'life of Jesus' (4:10–11). As their models had done, they had to take risks to assist others less fortunate than they. The urge to participate in the collection, therefore, came from the depths of their being as Christians. Even before the collection had been announced the Phillipians had seen the need to alleviate Paul's financial burden while he worked in other communities (Phil. 4:14–16). This spontaneous recognition of charity as the essence of Christianity won them a place in his affections to which no other community could aspire, and which merited them the accolade of 'partners in the gospel' (Phil. 1:5, 7). They made the good news something real and vital by demonstrating the power of grace.

Paul's joyful experience of authentic Christianity in Macedonia was intensified by the good news from Corinth. In addition to reporting that the Corinthians were eager to be reconciled with Paul (7:11), Titus must have mentioned that he had taken advantage of his warm reception (7:15) to remind them that they had done little to fulfil their commitment to participate in the collection. He could not have worked long with Paul without knowing the importance he attached to this project, and the Corinthians would have been eager to do anything that would re-establish them in the apostle's good grace. Paul, therefore, decides to take advantage of this favourable climate, and tells them that he is sending Titus back to Corinth (8:6). Even though Timothy was available (1:1), the one who had been the witness of their promises was the best placed to stimulate the move to performance.

The justification for this subtle form of pressure is clear in 8:7, where Paul finally comes to the point and reveals the conclusion which the Corinthians should draw from the example of the Macedonians. By praising their 'faith, speech, and knowledge' (cf. 1 Cor. 1:5) he begins with a *captio benevolentiae* which would have been flattering to the Corinthians but which for Paul was not a real compliment. These were spiritual gifts (1 Cor. 12:8–9) which some at Corinth, notably the Spirit-people, had exploited to selfish ends, and which did not rate very high on Paul's scale of values (cf. 1 Cor. 13). When he is being totally sincere he compliments a community on its faith, hope and charity (1 Thess. 1:3; 2 Thess. 1:3; Col. 1:4–5) or its partnership in the gospel (Phil. 1:5). Here he definitely has his tongue in his cheek, but at least he could find something good to say, whereas in the case of the Galatians he had been reduced to silence by their various improprieties.

The 'earnestness' of the Corinthians had been real when Titus left (7:11), and Paul had at first accepted it at face value. Money, however, has the effect of introducing a note of realism into even the most satisfying of illusions, and Paul here refuses to equate it with love. Against a number of modern translations the best text does not make Paul compliment the Corinthians on 'your love for us' (7:7; cf. 6:12); instead, he counts among *their* benefits 'our love for you' (cf. 2:4). Paul was not devoid of humour or subtlety, and we find here a delicate hint that the Corinthians have something to live up to.

It is his unfeigned affection (6:11) which permits him to exhort them 'see that you excel in this gracious work also' (8:7). The translation 'gracious work' is demanded by the context, but the word is elsewhere rendered 'grace'. The collection was to be a channel of divine aid which he hoped would not only alleviate the misery of the Jerusalem church, but would also open their eyes to the fact that God was also active among the gentiles. The Jerusalemites needed help to be convinced of the divine legitimacy of the mission to the gentiles.

The request is expressed in an imperatival form which could easily give the impression that Paul was imposing an obligation. This he immediately excludes: 'I say this not as a command' (8:8a). This is an extremely important clue to Paul's understanding of the function of moral imperatives, and it is not an isolated example. Equally concerning an act of charity, he tells Philemon that he will not order him to treat Onesimus as a brother in Christ (Philem. 8), and goes on to explain: 'I preferred to do nothing without your consent in order that your goodness might not be by compulsion but of your own free will' (Philem. 14). He gives the same reason here: 'Each one must do as he has made up his mind, not reluctantly or under compulsion, for God loves a cheerful giver' (9:7). To do something out of obedience cannot be an act of freedom. One cannot be 'bound' by a precept and free at the same time. If the donations to the collection were to have any value in Paul's eyes they had to be inspired by the donors' love. To make them mandatory would be to frustrate what he hoped would be an educational process leading to an authentic understanding of what it meant to be a Christian. The poor in Jerusalem might benefit financially, but a wonderful opportunity would have been lost.

This opportunity is the chance offered the Corinthians to show that the love they profess is in fact genuine (8:8b). The time for talking is over. In Christ they have been given a standard (5:15), and it has been concretized in the present and for this occasion in the behaviour of the Macedonians, who gave not only their money but themselves (8:4–5). To bring up the example of the Macedonians in this way carried the risk of turning the collection into a vulgar competition over who could give the most. Paul avoids this danger by bringing Christ into the picture (8:9).

His presentation of the ministry of Christ in terms of 'riches' and 'poverty' is unique in the New Testament. It has been widely interpreted as an allusion to the incarnation. The divine Word abandoned the riches of heaven in order to assume the poverty of human existence.[57] Such a meaning, however, has no basis either in Paul's general theological perspective or in the immediate context. The imagery of 'riches' and 'poverty' was suggested by the topic that Paul is discussing, but the underlying thought is that of 5:21, where the Sinless One is made 'sin'. The contrast is the same and in both cases it is motivated by concern for humanity. There is a difference in that in 5:21 God is the agent, whereas in 8:9 it is Christ. This, however, is a difference only in perspective. The same event is viewed first as an element in the divine plan of salvation and then in terms of indispensable human co-operation. A further parallel is furnished by the hymn cited by Paul in Philippians 2:6–11. Being 'in the form of God' Christ 'emptied himself taking the form of a slave' (Phil. 2:6–7), which is later specified as 'becoming obedient unto death, even death on a cross' (Phil. 2:8).

Christ therefore became 'poor' by accepting the radical impoverishment of a degrading and humiliating death in which everything was taken from him. Even though he was sinless, he accepted the punishment meted out to sinners. His 'riches', in consequence, can only mean his enjoyment of God's fellowship and his complete submission to his will. As 'the form of God', which is merely a synonym for 'the image of God' (Gen. 1:26–7), he was what God intended humanity to be, and so perfectly reconciled with God. This communion he gave up for the desolation of the cross.

A major advantage of this interpretation, which the incarnational meaning does not enjoy, is that it enables us to retain the same meanings for 'riches' and 'poverty' when they are

---

[57] So for example Furnish, *II Corinthians*, 417; and F. Dreyfus, *Did Jesus know he was God?* (Chicago, 1989), 55–6. J. D. G. Dunn, however, warns that 'we should be wary of assuming that the context of thought was an already established christology of incarnation. Would it have been so obvious to Paul's readers that he was speaking of the incarnation or of Christ's descent from heaven?' (*Christology in the Making. A New Testament Inquiry into the Origins of the Doctrine of the Incarnation* (London, 1980; 2nd edn 1989), 121). He rightly answers in the negative. Paul's meaning is to be sought in his Adamic christology.

transferred to the Corinthians. Prior to their conversion they were existentially 'dead' (2:16), and therefore 'poor' in the most radical sense. By their integration into the saving death of Christ through baptism they have acquired 'riches' by being reconciled with God (5:19) and enjoy his fellowship. The Corinthians 'knew' this grace communicated to them by Christ, but the knowledge remained theoretical. They must in practice 'live no longer for themselves but for him who for their sake died and was raised' (5:15). In the present context this means that they should demonstrate their love for others by participating in the collection. Having been made 'rich' through the grace of Christ, it is appropriate that they should share with others. This should be their real motive, not any desire to emulate the Macedonians.

Having clarified this issue, Paul returns to his persuasion of the Corinthians. In order to avoid any impression that he is giving them no choice, he deliberately introduces what he is going to say as his 'advice', and prefaces it by 'it is best' so as not to appear to criticize (8:10a). What was past was past and there was no point in highlighting their failure. He reminds them that twelve months ago they had been eager to participate in the collection (1 Cor. 16:1–4); they had agreed even before the Macedonians had joined the project (8:10b). Thus they should follow through on their commitment, and make their promises come true (8:11). Here we find Paul at his best in terms of religious leadership: he praises what can be praised (their willingness), and permits the Corinthians' self-respect to function as an internal incentive. In order to assuage any possible anxiety on their part as to the sum expected, he is at pains to emphasize that their attitude is more important than the value of their gift (8:12). A little given with a whole heart is more precious that a greater sum given grudgingly. It is not impossible that the Corinthians had intimated to Titus that they preferred to defer their particpation on the grounds that they could give more later. But this is rather speculative, and Paul's concern for their motive, the most important aspect of the collection in his eyes, is an adequate explanation for what he says.

If the Corinthians had only little to give, a donation might put them at risk. This drew Paul's attention to a possible objection: 'Why should we beggar ourselves in order that the members of the church in Jerusalem can live in luxury?' Patiently he points out that it is childish to think in terms of Corinthians and Jerusalemites changing places. He knows and they know that, however little they have, it is more than the poor of Jerusalem. Therefore, they should give now. In the future their situations might be reversed, and in that case they can expect aid from Jerusalem. In either case an equitable balance is maintained (8:13–14). The sort of thing he has in mind is illustrated, not demanded, by a citation of Exodus 16:18, which refers to the distribution of manna during the journey through the wilderness.

THE RECOMMENDATION OF REPRESENTATIVES (8:16–9:5)

Perhaps inspired by the experience of the Macedonians, whose zeal for the collection was certainly stimulated by the presence first of Timothy and then of Paul himself, Paul decides to send emissaries to Corinth to support his words by their exhortations. This was a delicate business, because it might look like pressure or interference in the internal matters of a local church, and Paul knew well how sensitive the Corinthians were. A slight embarrassment is evident in the way he writes.

Thus he begins by saying that he is not really sending Titus, as is implied in 8:6. His urging was totally unnecessary, because Titus himself was understandably keen to return in the light of what he took to be the success of his first mission (7:15). Paul's own love for the Corinthians had been kindled in the heart of his co-worker (8:16–17). This little vignette is illustrative of Paul's dealings with his assistants: he does not order a subordinate, but asks a 'partner' (8:23). His example inspired a similar vision and zeal, and once they perceived a problem they were prepared to act as Paul would. Such an attitude is indeed exemplary of how to lead and inspire those who are not themselves obliged to behave or act in the way that is suggested.

What has just been said might appear to be contradicted by the very next sentence, 'We are sending with him the renowned brother' (8:18a), but it is quickly made clear that this person-age was selected by the churches of Macedonia to act as their delegate in the actual assembling of the money for Jerusalem, and that all Paul is in fact doing is introducing him to the community. It is curious that, while his qualifications are given prominence, his name is never mentioned (8:18–19). Many explanations have been suggested, but in the light of the contacts between the Corinthian and Macedonian churches (11:9; 1 Thess. 1:7–8), the simplest hypothesis is that he was a Corinthian Christian, who had gone to aid the spread of the church in Macedonia, and who had there established himself as an exceptional preacher of the gospel. When the Corinthians recognized him and heard Paul's eulogy, they would have been both flattered and relieved. Their contribution to a sister church was publicly recognized, and Paul's emissary was not a critical Macedonian (9:4) but one of their own.

Election was not Paul's way of doing things; he preferred to recognize those who exhibited leadership by their practical dedication to the common good of the community (1 Cor. 16:16; 1 Thess. 5:12–13). His acceptance of the Macedonian procedure is indicative of the freedom he gave each of his communities. He would step in to challenge only when he felt that something was incompatible with the gospel, and even then he did not impose a solution, but forced further reflection on the part of the community by his arguments and observa-tions. It was up to each community to work out what Christian living meant in practice (cf. Phil. 1:9–10; Col. 1:9–10), and to remove this responsibility from it would be to rob it of its freedom.

The Macedonian envoy had been elected to travel with Paul in a 'ministry of grace', and his selection had the apostle's approval. His appointment was not to honour Paul, as a prime minister might accompany a visiting dignitary from the airport, but to give glory to God (8:19). The meaning of this rather strange phrase is made clear in the verses which follow. Paul knew that he was going to be responsible for a considerable sum of money, and that it was imperative, if his reputation (on which his witness depended) was to remain intact, not only that his motives should be pure, but that his actions should be impeccable in the sight of all (8:20–1). To be honest was not enough; he had to be seen to be honest, and this is where the envoy came in. He was to guarantee the integrity of the project, and thus to ensure that it in fact gave glory to God. Were the collection to be tarnished by suspicion and rumours it could not redound to God's glory. This precaution was an eminently sensible one, given the reputation of officials who had to deal with money, and at this point (but see 12:18) there is no reason to think that there were any at Corinth who thought that there was an element of fraud in the collection.

Titus and the envoy from Macedonia appear to have a higher status than a third who is to accompany them. The one quality that Paul singles out is his 'zealousness', which has been tested many times (8:22). This would appear to suggest that he was a long-time companion of Paul; note the contrast between 'our brother' and 'the brother' (8:18). If so, he could have been known to at least some of the Corinthians, which would explain why he is not named. Titus' 'zeal' for the Corinthians (8:17–17) was founded on his personal knowledge of the community, and there is no reason to think that this individual's zeal was based on second-hand reports.

Having introduced the three emissaries, Paul sums up their qualifications (8:23). Titus' status as 'my partner and co-worker in your regard' shows the esteem in which Paul held him, and which he had earned in his previous delicate mission to Corinth. The other two are described as 'apostles of the churches'. This is understandable for the envoy from Macedonia, but not for the other, because the impression given by 8:22 is that he was selected by Paul and not by the Macedonians. It may be that some other church had assigned him to work with Paul at an earlier stage in the latter's career. They are also called 'the glory of Christ', a qualification unique in the Pauline letters. They give glory to Christ by the quality of their lives (3:18), which are totally dedicated to 'the gospel of the glory of Christ' (4:4).

These three, then, represent a standard of Christian living which will challenge the Corinthians, and Paul begs the latter to live up to the reputation which he has given them (8:24). He asks for 'a demonstration of love'. This can hardly mean merely that they should welcome the envoys warmly. Simple hospitality is not so exceptional that it would make an impact on other churches. Of course, Paul expects that his envoys will be well received, but his concern is with the collection. If love becomes visible in the quality of an action which makes it beautiful, the Corinthians must not give grudgingly but in such a way as to show that their gift comes from an open and generous spirit (cf. 8:8). They must reveal themselves, not in the quantity of their gift, but in their attitude towards the recipients.

Paul knew perfectly well, however, that people can believe themselves open to others without actually doing anything positive. Hence, he reminds the Corinthians that he is not thinking in terms of their willingness to contribute to the collection. That is something he takes for granted, and so he does not need to write to them about that aspect (9:1). In fact, he has used their zeal to stimulate that of the people of Macedonia by proclaiming 'Achaia has been ready since last year' (9:2).

This unexpected reference to Achaia, the Roman province of which Corinth was the capital, has led some scholars to conclude that chapter 9 was originally a separate letter addressed to communities other than Corinth and of which Cenchreae is the only one known (Rom. 16:1). Since no other evidence recommends this hypothesis, it is more likely that the mention of Achaia was occasioned by the name of its sister province, Macedonia, and that Paul is actually thinking of Corinth. His claim is at best a half-truth, because he was fully aware that the Corinthians had, in fact, done nothing about the collection. In the euphoria following his reconciliation with them (7:16), however, he felt he had to emphasize the one aspect which he hoped was true. He may have been a little naive in this respect, but no matter what problems his communities caused him, he was loyal to them, and presented them in their best light to others.

If taking the will for the deed was an excusable supposition, it might nevertheless have unfortunate consequences should the Macedonians discover that the facts did not bear out the truth of what he had told them. Evidently, they had not yet decided on what procedure they would adopt to send their contribution to Jerusalem, but it was entirely possible that they would opt to have their representatives carry it to Corinth in Paul's company, and then go on with him to Jerusalem (9:4). In this scenario it would be extremely embarrassing for Paul to find that no money had been collected at Corinth (9:3). Thus he takes the precaution of sending ahead the three envoys (8:16–24) in order that the Corinthians might have fulfilled their pledge by the time he arrived.

To highlight the fact that Paul and the Corinthians might be humiliated before a much poorer church is a form of moral blackmail (9:4). Paul was desperate that the collection should succeed, but he was not prepared to pay too high a price. As usual, his good sense surfaces at the last minute, and he redeems himself by telling them that he does not want to 'extort' money from them (9:5). That would be self-defeating. If the collection is to forge a bond of love between the Jewish and gentile churches, it must be 'a blessing', that is, something given freely and spontaneously and inspired by goodwill towards others.

THE REWARDS OF GENEROSITY (9:6–15)

Aware of the pitfall which he has just escaped, Paul moves resolutely into a strictly theological mode in order to exhort the Corinthians to be liberal in their generosity.

The first part of his appeal (9:6–10) is dominated by agricultural imagery. In itself this is rather surprising because Paul grew up in a city, Tarsus (Acts 21:39), and Pharisaism, which he joined in Jerusalem (Phil. 3:5), was an urban movement. He can have had little, if any, direct experience of farm life, yet the imagery deriving therefrom plays a surprisingly prominent part in his metaphorical world. It has been plausibly suggested that Paul was influenced by the parables of Jesus,[58] but such imagery is also common in wisdom literature and permeates certain sections of ancient classical literature.[59] Thus, though he could have made the same point by speaking of investment, which would have been more suited to the milieu at Corinth, there can be little doubt that his principle would have been easily understood (9:6).

The principle that what one will harvest is proportionate to what one has sown (9:6) is true only under ideal conditions, i.e. in the absence of disease or natural disasters, which no one can guarantee. Paul, of course, does not intend that his words be taken literally. He is trying to tempt the Corinthians to give generously, and this is perfectly clear in the Greek because the phrase translated 'bountifully' (*ep' eulogiais*) is based on his designation of their gift as a 'blessing' (*eulogia*) in 9:5. One might paraphrase rather awkwardly: 'The more blessings you give, the more you will receive.'

He immediately adds a condition: the attitude of the giver is all-important; it must be a genuinely free decision rooted in the core of the donor's being. If it is tinged with reluctance or the result of external pressure it will not be valued by God (9:7). Little with gladness, therefore, is better than much with a heavy heart. In saying that 'God loves a cheerful giver' Paul appears to have in mind Proverbs 22:8a (LXX), 'God blesses a cheerful and generous person', which he modified in the light of Proverbs 22:11, 'The Lord loves pious hearts.' The verb 'to bless' would have carried on the thought of 9:6 more precisely, and would have led most appropriately into what follows. If Paul substituted 'to love' it can only be because he wants to say something more about the attitude of the giver. A gift which is given in love draws forth love in return; donor and recipient are united in the exchange. It is hard to feel even gratitude for a gift which is given unwillingly or with hesitation.

---

[58] H. Riesenfeld, 'Le Langage parabolique dans les épîtres de saint Paul', in A. Descamps (ed.) *Litérature et théologie Pauliniennes* (RechBib 5; Brugge, 1960), 47–59.
[59] Multiple references are given by Furnish, *II Corinthians*, 440.

Why does Paul bring God into the picture? The connection he makes would be simple enough if the collection were like the temple tax, which was considered as given to God, but we have seen that this was not the case. It was destined to relieve the poverty of a segment of the Jerusalem community, and it would have been natural to evoke their response, particularly in view of the bridge-building object of the collection. Fundamentally, however, the collection was to be an expression of authentic love (8:8), which actualized the very being of the believers (1 Cor. 13:2). Only by loving did they live in such a way as to please God (1 Thess. 4:1). Hence, even though directed to other human beings, any act of true love had a relationship to God.

Another consideration is important if the relationship to the next verse is to be understood. It was widely believed that material prosperity was the result of divine beneficence: 'God richly furnishes us with everything to enjoy' (1 Tim. 6:17). Thus the 'self-sufficiency' that the Corinthians enjoy is the effect of God's grace (9:8). Their needs are comfortably met, but this does not mean that they can luxuriate in their blessings. Wealth is not given by God to be hoarded, but to be used, and not only in one's own self-interest. Jesus succinctly summed up the general understanding of the obligation of wealth: 'Freely you have received, freely give' (Matt. 6:10). Thus the 'cheerful giver' is one who recognizes the purpose of God's gift, and who is loved by him for such practical knowledge.

This is why Paul goes on to specify that the purpose of the God-given self-sufficiency of the Corinthians is that they should 'abound in every good work' (9:8). The best commentary is that of the author of 1 Timothy, who says that the obligation of wealth is 'to do good, to be rich in beautiful works, to be magnificently generous, to have a developed sense of community' (6:18). Good works are not the cause of grace, but its effect. The ability to perform such works comes from God, and they do not justify us in his eyes.

How the citation of Psalms 112(111):9 fits into the argument (9:9) is not entirely clear, because it can be taken in two ways.

In its literal sense it praises the just man who gives generously to the poor, and who in consequence remains in the state of righteousness conferred on him by God. In this sense it functions as an implicit exhortation to the Corinthians to contribute to the collection for the poor; this is the principal 'good work' that Paul has in mind. The only difficulty with this interpretation is that it creates a serious problem regarding the transition to 9:10. The two parts of this latter verse strongly suggest that it is a commentary on the citation in 9:9, and the commentary identifies the subject of the citation as God, which fits with 9:8. Hence, the context demands the assumption that Paul here cites Psalms 112(111):9 in a transferred sense. The acts of the just man are taken as acts of God, and this is in fact justified by the Old Testament, because in the psalter Psalms 111(110) and 112(111) are a pair, as their alphabetical construction indicates, and the first psalm praises God's works, which are understood as the basis of those of the just man in the second.

The idea of 'scattering' in the psalm evoked the action of the sower, and is interpreted by an allusion to Isaiah 55:10–11: 'For as the rain and snow come down from heaven, and return not thither but water the earth, making it bring forth and sprout, giving seed to the sower and bread to the eater' (9:10a). Without God's gift of rain there would be no crop, which provides seed for the following year and grain to be milled for flour. The theme of God as the ultimate provider recalls 9:8, and is here developed into the future. If God has given so generously in the past, he will continue to do so in the future: 'he will supply and multiply your resources' (9:10b). An unstated condition, however, is implicit in the context. The Corinthians must use what they have in the way that God intended: namely, by sharing it with those who have less. The word translated as 'resources' is literally 'seed', which remains sterile unless it is scattered. Thus they will reap 'the fruits of righteousness' (9:10c; cf. Hosea 10:12). It is not that they thereby make themselves righteous, but are given the opportunity of showing their right status before God. They will be recognized as conforming to God's will.

The underlying principle in this argument is: the more you give, the more you will get from God. Is this really true? Experience answers in the negative. A businessman who uses his profits to assist the Third World instead of paying his taxes will end up with a heavy fine or a jail sentence. In a famine area the only consequence of a mother's giving all available food to her children is that she will die more quickly. Those who impoverish themselves in giving to the poor will find themselves eating in soup kitchens. The realities of life were no different in the first century, and Paul knew it. He gave to the utmost, and what were the results? 'Toil and hardship, many a sleepless night, hunger and thirst, cold and exposure' (11:27).

Are we to assume, then, that Paul was an unscrupulous liar, who made false promises in order to induce the Corinthians to part with their cash? Such an assessment fails to appreciate the idealism of his presuppositions. Paul is assuming that believers are authentic, and not merely nominal, Christians. He also takes for granted that God's gifts are given through human channels. Finally, he presumes that each local church is a genuine community, and that the various communities are united by bonds of love. This is the context out of which he speaks with the certitude of hope. His optimism has not been eroded by his experience of individuals and churches which fail to live up to the ideal. Christians who put themselves at risk through their generosity will be aided by others who notice their situation and come to their assistance. Similarly, one community will look out for another and ensure that it does not go under financially. These are the human channels through which God communicates his benefits. It is not that God fails those who trust in him; any failure is on the side of Christians who have been trusted by God. Believers who challenge Paul's general principle only succeed in calling into question their own incipient laziness and lack of charity. Those inspired to be generous should be able to give without worry, secure in the knowledge that others have been entrusted by God with their care. Such is the freedom of the children of God.

Thus Paul continues 'you are enriched in every way for all forms of generosity' (9:11a). The fact that the Corinthians had more than was adequate for their needs was a sign from God that he had a purpose for the excess. Through Paul's appeal for the poor of Jerusalem they have become aware of what that purpose is, and if they fulfil it, 'thanksgiving will rise to God' from those whose misery has been alleviated (9:11b). This concept underlines Paul's understanding of the role of the Corinthians as instrumental in the execution of God's plan. God is to be thanked because it was he who, through a series of human instruments, gave them the insight and the means to respond to the situation in Jerusalem. This is not to say that the Jerusalemites will fail to acknowledge the sacrifices involved in the Corinthians' 'ministry of public service' (9:12); on the contrary, their gratitude will be expressed in love and prayer (9:14). They will long to be united with their benefactors and will beg for them all blessings. On a much more fundamental level, however, they will recognize that it is God's grace (9:14) which has enabled the Corinthians' 'profession of faith in the gospel of Christ' to be true 'obedience' and not an empty verbal formula (9:13).

Paul here perceives the ideal result of the collection, and cries: 'Thanks be to God for his indescribable gift' (9:15). Not only will the Corinthians be inspired to an expression of authentic Christianity, but the Jerusalemites will recognize that God's grace is active in those who come from another racial stock, and whose attitude towards the Mosaic Law differed radically from theirs. Both of these happy occasions still lie in the future; they represent a goal towards which he is still working. The energy which drives him is his conviction that he has been chosen by God to find a way of demonstrating the fundamental unity of the two branches of the church of Christ. Although he could, God will not act directly in history, because he has decided to do so indirectly, through human representatives. Their insight into the problem, their initiative in finding solutions, their perseverance in putting them into effect, are all essential to the working of grace within an historical context. This is why Paul can think of himself and his collaborators as 'God's co-workers' (1 Cor. 3:6). His concern for the collection is a perfect illustration of his awareness that God depends on human co-operation to touch, to move, to illuminate and to heal.

CHAPTER 7

What went wrong at Corinth?

As noted in the introduction (pp. 10–12), chapters 10–13 (Letter B) cannot be the continuation of chapters 1–9 (Letter A). The rather calculating confidence displayed by Paul in Letter A gives way to an attitude of complete frustration in Letter B. The reasonable tone and subtle arguments of Letter A are replaced by a wild outburst in which Paul gives his capacity for sarcasm and irony free rein. What went wrong at Corinth in the few months that separated the two letters?

Letter A, it will be remembered, had two fundamental objectives: to drive a wedge between the Judaizers and the Spirit-people; and to win the latter to Paul's side. The secondary character of the appeal for the collection is shown by the fact that Paul raises this issue only at the very end, when he hoped that the body of the letter would have had its effect. How well Paul succeeded with the Spirit-people is an open question, but it appears that he did achieve his goal of isolating the Judaizers. Having lost what they hoped would be their constituency at Corinth, the Judaizers could only redouble their attacks on Paul's position and authority. If there was now little chance of converting the Spirit-people to Judaeo-Christianity, there remained the possibility that they would still be receptive to criticism of Paul. The basic issue of Letter B, therefore, is Paul's ministry.

The old criticism of his unimpressive presence and uninspired preaching is dragged up again, and Letter A gave them new ammunition. The importance which Paul attached to the collection gave them the opportunity to highlight what they presented as his suspiciously ambiguous attitude towards money. On the one hand, Paul had refused to accept money for himself (1 Cor. 9:1–18), but on the other hand he had twice solicited the Corinthians for funds for a church whose need they had to take on faith (1 Cor. 16:1–4; 2 Cor. 8–9). The distinction is perfectly clear, and Paul's attitude is in fact entirely consistent. Yet it was not too difficult for the Judaizers to muddy the waters.

It would have been easy for them simply to shrug their shoulders when the Corinthians questioned them about the poverty of the Jerusalem church. They did not have to tell an outright lie by denying any need for the collection. All that they had to do was subtly to hint that the questioners were being naive in taking Paul's statements at face value. It would also have been easy for them to misrepresent his refusal to accept support from the Corinthians, particularly since he had made a bad mistake in dealing with this issue in 1 Corinthians.

Paul's renunciation of financial aid while at Corinth was motivated by his belief that this enhanced his witness value. His disinterest in money not only differentiated him from charlatans who sold knowledge, but it enhanced his credibility. He preached because he was convinced he had been chosen to do so, not out of any self-interest on his part. The existential aspect of his behaviour gave force to what he proclaimed. It is also possible that Paul wanted to preserve his liberty to move elsewhere when he considered the community to be sufficiently well established. He cannot have been unaware of the convention, wide-spread in the Roman world, that acceptance of financial aid instituted a patron–client relationship which limited the freedom of the client.[60]

This refusal to accept what in the first century was thought of as a perfectly normal relationship could be presented in a very different light by the Judaizers. In Roman society, and Corinth was a Roman colony, the litmus test of prestige and social standing was the size and number of one's benefactions.

[60] The importance of this social relationship for a correct understanding of 2 Corinthians 10–13 is correctly emphasized by V. P. Furnish (*II Corinthians* (AB; Garden City, NY, 1984), 506–9). For a survey of the more important works on the topic, see J. H. Elliott, 'Patronage and Clientism in Early Christian Society. A Short Reading List', *Forum* 3/4 (1987), 39–48.

One could grace a city with statues or beautiful buildings and/or assist a number of needy clients, be they poets, artists or simply hangers-on. For the Corinthians to offer money to Paul was a socially acceptable way of affirming the power and influence of the community to which they belonged. By such a gesture they also proffered friendship. Such expectations gave the Judaizers a very strong case. They could point out that Paul did not really love the Corinthians, as he professed, because he had spurned their friendship. They could also emphasize that he belittled the whole community in refusing it the prestige which it merited. Finally, they could insist that Paul had lied to the community by giving the impression that he earned his own living at Corinth (1 Cor. 9:15–18), while all the time he had been receiving money secretly from Macedonia (2 Cor. 11:7–9). In other words, given the conventions of the time, he had preferred to be a client of Macedonia, and his behaviour was nothing but a studied insult to the Corinthian church.

By worldly standards this was a reasonable interpretation of Paul's attitude, and it did his standing in the community serious damage. To Paul, who operated by other standards, it appeared as malicious distortion of his motives. His bitter anger was intensified by the knowledge that, if he was discredited, his version of the gospel was at risk, and another gospel might take its place. A desperate anxiety for the future of the Corinthian community he had nourished fuelled the passion that burns through this letter.[61]

---

[61] As is often the case, such anger reveals an unexpected facet of the personality. Paul had erected a facade of rhetorical inadequacy (1 Cor. 2:1–5; 2 Cor. 10:10; 11:6), which here crumbles to expose him as a highly skilled orator with a developed 'understanding of the forms of logical argument and refutation, the deliberate arrangement of material, and the careful choice and composition of words' (G. A. Kennedy, *New Testament Interpretation through Rhetorical Criticism* (Chapel Hill, 1984), 96). For the depth of Paul's insertion into his literary environment see in particular H. D. Betz, *Der Apostel Paulus und die sokratische Tradition. Eine Exegetische Untersuchung zu seiner 'Apologie' 2 Kor 10–13* (BHT 45; Tubingen, 1972); and C. Forbes, 'Comparison, Self-Praise and Irony: Paul's Boasting and the Conventions of Hellenistic Rhetoric', *NTS* 32 (1986), 1–30. Since it is improbable that Paul simply 'picked up' such skills (a suggestion of F. Young and D. F. Ford, *Meaning and Truth in 2 Corinthians* (London, 1987), 41), it would seem that he must have had a good classical education.

CHAPTER 8

Paul takes the offensive (10:1–18)

Given Paul's frame of mind, it is very improbable that this letter began with a thanksgiving or a benediction. As in Galatians, he could find nothing in the community to inspire gratitude, and so goes straight to the heart of the matter. He does not, however, lash out wildly; his rage is well under control and makes him icily incisive.

During his second visit to Corinth Paul had not made an impressive showing, and his failure to return as he had promised (1:16, 23; 2:1) was presented as fear of confrontation. Hence, the jibe that he was abject when present, and forceful only when at a safe distance (10:1b, 10). Paul's reply is that he exhibited 'the meekness and gentleness of Christ' (10:1a), which can be understood on two different levels.

He had not reacted in the way which might be expected of a normal self-respecting person, because he refused to conform to the conventions of the world. His standard is Christ (5:16), and his concern is to exhibit in his comportment 'the life of Jesus' (4:10–11), who proclaimed himself to be 'gentle and lowly in heart' (Matt. 11:29). Paul knew a lot about the historical Jesus, and it is perfectly possible that he is thinking of episodes in the earthly ministry when Jesus exhibited kindness and forbearance.[62] He could not have exhorted the Corinthians to imitate him as he imitated Christ (1 Cor. 11:1) unless he had a very concrete image of the way Jesus behaved.

---

[62] See my 'What Paul knew of Jesus', *ScrB* 12 (1981), 35–40. There is no justification for V. P. Furnish's assertion that Paul is here thinking of the gracious condescension of the incarnate life of the pre-existent Lord (*II Corinthians* (AB; Garden City, NY, 1984), 460).

Thus, despite his feelings when insulted at Corinth, he treated the members of the church with love and forbearance. Despite serious provocation, he continued to preach by his example. He was his ministry.

The Corinthians, however, should not interpret his behaviour as weakness. He had acted out of conviction, not out of cowardice. In focusing on the externals, they had failed to penetrate beneath the surface to the reality of his ministry as grounded in the power of God (Rom. 1:16). 'Meekness and gentleness' characterized the historical Jesus, but 'meekness' is also a quality of the Messianic king (Zech. 9:9; cf. Matt. 21:5), and 'gentleness' is predicted of God (Wis. 12:18; 2 Macc. 2:22; 10:4). Since the nature of God is love (1 John 4:8, 16), his power is fundamentally a beneficent force, but the lesson of the history of salvation is that it can also be used to punish. As one chosen by God to execute his will in history, Paul is endowed with this divine power, but he wants to use it in a life-giving way, not to deal out death.

The complicated language of 10:2 betrays Paul's dilemma. His opponents at Corinth refuse to accept his faith-vision of ministry and authentic Christian life, but to crush them by force would obscure the true nature of the gospel as a message of love. While chastisement can be an expression of love, on the community level it is easily seen as vindictiveness towards those who think otherwise than the authorities. To those who have not been weaned fully from the perspectives of the world it appears to be no different to the exercise of political power. To act as a tyrant, therefore, would destroy Paul's conformity to Christ and totally compromise his witness.

The way he resolved his dilemma was to be harsh verbally and loving existentially. His threats were designed to crack the shell of complacency which enveloped some at Corinth, so that they could begin to learn what it really meant to be a Christian. It is doubtful if he ever intended to put them into practice. Certainly, on his second visit he did not put into effect the sanctions with which he had menaced the Corinthians in 1 Corinthians 4:18–21a. When present, he displayed only 'love in a spirit of gentleness' (1 Cor. 4:21b). His approach exhibited a Christ-like logic, but there was sufficient ambiguity for those who wished to accuse him of acting in a manipulative 'worldly fashion' (10:2), particularly if they also had his financial affairs in mind.

In reply, Paul makes a fundamental distinction (10:3): he is 'in the flesh' but he does not operate 'according to the flesh'. 'In the flesh' simply affirms the facticity of human existence. The physical dimension means that a person exists under specific conditions of space and time which create his or her world. To be 'in the flesh', therefore, is equivalent to existing 'in the world'. Social life 'in the world', however, is dominated by a false value system, which makes the individual the focus of all his or her striving. Thus to live 'according to the flesh' is to make one's own interest, power or prestige matters of ultimate concern; it is 'to belong to the world' (cf. Col. 2:20). The antithesis is to live 'according to the spirit' (Rom. 8:4), which means practical acceptance of the values lived by Christ (5:15).

Here Paul does not simply say that he lives 'according to the spirit', because he is in the midst of a battle for the salvation of the Corinthian community. He develops a military metaphor in which he appears as a general en route to attack a strongly defended city (10:4–6).[63] The credibility of the implicit threat lies in what he has already achieved in other campaigns, and in consequence the metaphor is revelatory of his ministry as a whole.

Just as a city is a 'stronghold' defended by 'great towers', so the minds of fallen humanity strive to protect themselves by 'reasonings' and 'thoughts' against 'the knowledge of God', which in practice means 'obedience to Christ' (10:4–5). The portrait of fallen humanity that is only sketched here is fully developed in Romans 1:18–32, where the intellectual and moral evils of society are traced back to a failure to honour God. Rather than discern the face and plan of God 'in the things he created', they used their intelligence to distort the purpose of creation and to justify values radically opposed to the authentic development of humanity. Paul's mission is to

---

[63] This interpretation has been worked out in detail by A. J. Malherbe, 'Antisthenes and Odysseus and Paul at War', *HTR* 76 (1983), 143–73.

break down these defences, not in order to establish his own power, but in order to re-establish the sovereignty of God, whose agent he is and whose power he wields. God, however, is no longer revealed only in his creation. Christ as the human face of God is the definitive manifestation of the divine plan for humanity. In consequence, Paul will not rely on 'persuasive words of wisdom' to demolish the reasons developed by fallen humanity to defend its values, but devotes all his energy to the presentation of 'Jesus Christ and him crucified' (1 Cor. 2:1–5). Authentic knowledge of God is 'obedience to Christ', i.e. lived acceptance of the fundamental value of love manifested in the surrender of self in the 'dying of Jesus' (4:10; cf. 5:15).

The language of the military metaphor is also highly relevant to the situation at Corinth. The Spirit-people had emphasized theoretical 'knowledge' at the expense of lived commitment, and the Judaizers had down-played the unique role of Christ by insisting on the Mosaic Law as a mediator of the knowledge of God. Recognition of the fact that the focus of opposition to Paul could be distinguished from the community as a whole is indispensable for a correct understanding of 10:2 and 6. Paul has a certain confidence that 'your obedience' will be complete (10:6), because the silent majority is more likely to trust him than to side with his adversaries, particularly in view of the reconciliation celebrated in his previous letter. Only if some persist in their 'disobedience' (10:6) will he have to 'summon up courage' to move against them when he comes (10:2). The hint that he hopes not to have to do so is an implicit appeal to the community to accept responsibility for its own authenticity both with regard to the purity of its gospel and with regard to the genuineness of its founder's ministry. It was a fundamental principle of Paul's pastoral theology that each local church was autonomous. It had to work out its own faith-vision and give it appropriate practical expression. Paul's role was to force it to rethink issues where he was convinced the community had made a wrong decision, not to provide authoritative solutions (cf. 1 Cor. 5). In the present case the primary responsibility for dealing with those who would subvert the true gospel and Paul's ministry lay with the

Corinthians. The community had moved from the passive stance, which they had adopted during the confrontation that marked his second visit, to siding with Paul (7:5–16). Now they have to take a step further and deal with the disruptive elements in their midst: 'Be alert to what is right in front of you!' (10:7a).

In order to give the obedient Corinthians arms in this task (5:12) Paul first responds to specific criticism stemming from his opponents (10:7–11), and then proceeds to attack them for lacking true authority and being out of their jurisdiction (10:12–18). The section is highly polemic, but, as always with Paul, what he says is rooted in a profoundly theological vision of his ministry.

Since it was true of all Christians (1 Cor. 3:23), the opponents' claim to be 'of Christ' must have had a very specific connotation for them (10:7b). The most plausible suggestion is that they were claiming to have been commissioned by Jesus during his earthly ministry or at least by some of his original disciples.[64] This, they felt, gave them a special authority superior to that of Paul. This clue that they belonged to the Jerusalem church is confirmed by the further hint that they were operating outside their proper territory (10:14–16) because at the Jerusalem conference it had been decided that, while Paul would go to the gentiles, the Jerusalem church would limit itself to the Jews (Gal. 2:9). Thus it is most probable that Paul here has the Judaizers in mind. In order to win a footing among the Spirit-people at Corinth they had to adopt the protective colouring of Hellenistic orators, and it was this that led them to adopt a secular comparative standard (impressive bearing, eloquent speech) to underpin their authority (10:12).

Paul gives no importance to the historical priority of the Jerusalem church, the dominant figure in whose leadership at this time was the highly conservative James, the brother of the

---

[64] The various possibilities of meaning are discussed by C. K. Barrett (*The Second Epistle to the Corinthians* (BNTC: London, 1973), 256–7) and Furnish (*II Corinthians*, 476), both of whom tend towards the interpretation adopted here.

Lord, who had not been a disciple during the lifetime of Jesus (Gal. 2:11; John 7:5). Any relationship, direct or indirect, to the historical Jesus was irrelevant. Paul's authority derived from his encounter with, and commissioning by, the Risen Christ (1 Cor. 9:1), and it was given him for 'building up' (10:8; cf. 13:10; Jer. 1:10), that is, for the establishment of new communities and for strengthening their understanding of the gospel. The ultimate credit, therefore, must go to God (10:17; cf. Jer. 9:24), and it is his approval alone that counts (10:18). The two allusions to Jeremiah indicate that Paul sees his function in God's plan as comparable to that of the prophets of the Old Testament (cf. Gal. 1:15 = Jer. 1:5). He speaks for God and he is accountable only to God. The judgement of the world and of those who conform to its standards is of no relevance (1 Cor. 4:1–4). At first sight this appears as the height of arrogance and as the justification for uncontrolled use of power by ecclesiastical authorities. For Paul, however, the gospel was new and different. God through Christ has revealed himself in a way that flatly contradicted the standards of the world (1 Cor. 1:20–5). In consequence, any attempt to make ministers credible in worldly terms or to make the gospel acceptable in terms of worldly conventions endangered the power of the cross (1 Cor. 1:17). Faith must be rooted in the power of the Spirit, and not in the 'wisdom' of men (1 Cor. 2:4–5). Ministers must meet the standards of the gospel. They must measure up to the criterion revealed in the comportment of Christ (5:15). They should not adapt themselves to popular demand, or vaunt their acceptability as a sign of evangelistic competence. Those who do so simply do not understand the nature of Christian ministry (10:12).

Paul's criticism of the Judaizers in terms of jurisdiction at first sight appears to be a legalistic argument (10:13–18). They were outside their territory and therefore in the wrong. On the *ad hominem* level it might have been convincing as far as the Corinthians were concerned, but it would have cut little ice with the Judaizers, who would have found it easy to refute. Since Paul was anything but a fool, the real argument must operate on another level and, not surprisingly, it is intimately related to his understanding of how ministry is to achieve its goal.

At the Jerusalem conference Paul and the Judaizers agreed that he should go 'to the nations', i.e. the gentiles, and they 'to the circumcision' (Gal. 2:9). In 10:13–18 Paul appears to assume that this agreement should be understood geographically, but the wording does not bear him out. The strict letter of the text grants a mandate to the Judaizers to convert Jews without any territorial restriction. In the first century the vast majority of Jews lived in the diaspora. Of the 6 million Jews in the Roman empire only about 400,000 lived in Palestine. Thus the Judaizers could very reasonably have claimed that they would have been failing to live up to the agreement by limiting their missionary activity to the inhabitants of the Holy Land. Moreover, on the basis of the promise to Abraham, 'in you shall all the families of the earth be blessed' (Gen. 12:3), they could have insisted that they had not only the right but also the obligation to preach their gospel among pagans. The Judaizers, therefore, had a strong case for their missionary presence in the diaspora.[65]

The human side of Paul's objection to their activity at Corinth is easy to grasp. He had been the first to evangelize the Corinthians (10:14c), and elementary morality rejects the attempt of others to profit by his labours (10:15–16). If he had done the spadework of tilling and planting (cf. 1 Cor. 3:6), what right had others to steal his crop?

There was also a theological objection. The mere fact that a church existed at Corinth demonstrated the activity of divine grace (3:1–3; cf. 1 Cor. 9:1–2), but Paul knew that the disputes and divisions within the community severely diminished its witness value (1 Cor. 10:32). Corinth was not a force in the spread of the gospel as were the churches at Philippi and Thessalonica (1 Thess. 1:6–8; Phil. 2:14–16). Even if the Judaizers did not poach Paul's converts, the situation at

---

[65] The common view that Jewish–Christian missionaries ventured outside Palestine only in order to counteract the Law-free ministry of Paul has been convincingly demolished by J. L. Martyn, 'A Law-Observant Mission to Gentiles: The Background of Galatians', *Michigan Quarterly Review* 22 (1983), 221–36.

Corinth would worsen drastically if they set up a Law-observant church in the city. Instead of being attracted by the visibility of love in action, outsiders would be confused by the two forms of Christianity and repelled by the animosity between the two groups.

Paul envisaged the collection for the poor of Jerusalem as an act of love which would draw the two branches of the wider church together. It was to be a practical demonstration that they were united at a deeper level and that their differences were only superficial. Until the problem was resolved in a way that would existentially reinforce the preaching of the gospel, common sense indicated that the Jewish and gentile missions should not interfere with one another in a way that made the task of each more difficult. They should not compete for converts, and they should not even be present in the same area. Thus, at the root of Paul's geographical interpretation of the Jerusalem agreement (Gal. 2:9) is his conviction that each local church should, by the quality of its Christianity, 'hold forth the word of life' (Phil. 2:16). This to him was so obvious that he thought that the Judaizers should have seen it in the same light. At best, their failure to do so indicated that they had failed to grasp the critical existential dimension of the mission of Christ in the world, and Christianity risked being devalued to a mere system of ideas overlaid on traditional Judaism. At worst, it suggested that their motivation was envy of Paul's success and that their mission was essentially destructive (10:8). In neither scenario could they manifest 'the life of Jesus' (4:10–11), which was the only authentic proclamation of the gospel.

CHAPTER 9

The Fool's Speech (11:1–12:13)

This section of Letter B is dominated by the words 'fool, foolish and foolishness' (11:1; 16, 17, 19, 21; 12:6, 11). Paul so characterizes what he is doing here, because it is precisely that for which he has just condemned his opponents. They boast of their spiritual prowess and compare themselves with one another (10:12, 18), and now he does likewise. He knows that he is being facetious, both because such boasting is intrinsically self-defeating, and because he is conscious that he was taking the risk of confirming the opinion that he was inconsistent (1:17). Yet he felt that he had no option. He had to stop the Judaizers and he had to restore his credibility with the Spirit-people. Only one dangerous tactic would do both, a display of his rhetorical ability.

The Judaizers had made their mark at Corinth by clever personal propaganda. In reply, Paul attacks the whole idea of self-advertisement by a parody which exhibits a profound knowledge of its methods.[66] By means of sharp sarcasm and subtle irony he makes the procedure appear ridiculous. The Spirit-people, on the other hand, had disparaged his speaking ability, and compared him unfavourably with Apollos (10:10b). He hopes that this display of his knowledge of rhetorical conventions will convince them that his mode of preaching was by choice and not by necessity. He deliberately opted to appear 'unskilled in speech' (11:6) so that his hearers would focus on the essential message 'Jesus Christ and him crucified' (1 Cor. 2:2) and on the existential reinforcement of

---

[66] See in particular C. Forbes 'Comparison, Self-Praise and Irony: Paul's Boasting and the Conventions of Hellenistic Rhetoric', *NTS* 32 (1986), 1–30.

his comportment that exhibited 'the life of Jesus' (4:10–11). If he had failed to help them to see this in Letter A he had to adopt a different approach and reveal more of his background than he had previously thought relevant. He had had a very good classical education in Tarsus, which was famed for its schools (Strabo, *Geography* 14:5.13), and had to show that it was equal if not superior to theirs. If he could force them to ask why he had not displayed it, he felt that he had a chance of their appreciating his understanding of authentic ministry and how it should achieve its goal.

PAUL'S JUSTIFICATION FOR BEING FOOLISH (11:1–21A)

The Spirit-people and the Judaizers were only a portion of the community at Corinth. Paul also had to take into account the main body of the church, and he is gravely concerned as to how they would react to this departure from his normal mode of communication. Like anyone who consciously sets out to play the fool he is embarrassed, and this nervousness betrays itself in a rather verbose introduction; he actually starts boasting only in 11:21b. He feels that he has to explain, to justify his behaviour. He is 'deeply concerned' about them (11:2a) and the subtle danger that menaces them forces him to take extraordinary measures.

He begins by defining his relationship to the community in terms of Jewish marriage custom, according to which the bride's father is responsible for safeguarding her virginity until he escorts her to the bridegroom's house. For Paul to describe himself as the father of the community is much more than a metaphor for his loving attitude towards it. He had begotten it through the gospel (1 Cor. 4:15). He had been the providential agent through whom God had given its members 'life' in the existential sense: 'From him you "are" in Christ Jesus' (1 Cor. 1:30). By accepting the gospel the Corinthians had committed themselves totally and irrevocably to Christ, but they would be united fully with him only at his Second Coming (1 Thess. 4:16–17). In the interval it was Paul's responsibility to ensure that they lived up to the engagement implicit in their baptism.

The Old Testament imagery of Israel as the betrothed of Yahweh (Isa. 54:5–6; 62:5; Ezek. 16:8; Hos. 2:19–20) certainly influenced Paul's concept of the church as the bride of Christ (11:2).[67] The aspect of complete dedication guarantees continuity, but there is also a radical discontinuity. Yahweh was totally other, and was known only through perfect obedience to his Law. Jesus Christ, on the contrary, was the human face of God revealed in history, and who continued to be manifested in the comportment of Paul, who displayed 'the life of Jesus' (4:10–11). The community's acceptance of him as the model of authentic human existence implied submission to a demand at once more exigent and more liberal that that of the Law. No longer is it a question of read and obey. Now one has to discern in freedom and full responsibility what conformity to Christ requires in the multifarious circumstance of life.

This requirement of continuous search and discovery, which is intrinsic to authentic Christian existence, created the possibility that the Corinthians might be 'deceived' (11:3). Paul does not fear that they will abandon the faith, but that they will be 'seduced' from the clear vision of Christ which he had presented to them both in word and deed (5:15). The imminence of the danger is highlighted by the fact that the Judaizers presented themselves and their message in terms identical with those he himself employed. They were 'apostles of Christ' (11:13), and their 'gospel' concerned both 'Jesus' and the 'Spirit' (11:4). On this verbal level they were indistinguishable from Paul! The difference lies in the content they give these terms, and this is the critical element as far as Paul is concerned.

Unfortunately, he does not tell us precisely what their teaching was, but a shrewd guess can be made on the basis of the opposition we know he is facing. He uses the phrase 'another gospel' elsewhere only in Galatians 1:6, where, as the whole tenor of that letter makes clear, it is question of a version

---

[67] Paul's application of this image to the Corinthian church, in which women certainly exercised leadership roles (1 Cor. 11:2–16; Rom. 16:1–2) means that Eph. 5:21–33 cannot be used as the basis of an ecclesiology which would exclude women from ordination. It is so used in the 1988 Apostolic Letter of Pope John Paul II, *Mulieris Dignitatem*, nn. 23–7.

of the good news that gives supreme importance to acceptance of circumcision and observance of the Law. This, of course, automatically reduces the salvific role of 'Jesus' to insignificance. To Paul a Jesus who is essentially irrelevant is certainly 'another Jesus'. Finally, in counterdistinction to their approach in Galatia, the Judaizers highlight the 'Spirit' in order to forge a bond with the Spirit-people for whom the Spirit was but another name for Wisdom (Philo, *De Gigantibus* 23). What precisely it meant for the Judaizers remains obscure, but it was certainly 'another Spirit' for Paul, who thought of the Holy Spirit as the inspiration emanating from a community totally committed to following the example of the self-giving Christ (5:15).[68]

By not specifying the precise difference between his understanding of the gospel and that of his opponents, Paul throws down the gauntlet to the Corinthians, and indulges in an aside directed to the Spirit-people, who criticized Paul's speaking ability (10:10) and prided themselves on their 'knowledge' (1 Cor. 8:1). Following Philo, they believed that eloquence was integral to the possession of wisdom (*De Migratione* 70–3), but in practice assumed that verbal facility implied superior religious insight. Conceding that his oratory is defective by worldly standards (through choice, not necessity), Paul notes that he is 'not unskilled in knowledge' (11:6). The implication is that he at least could distinguish the genuine from the spurious both as regards the meaning of the gospel and the status of the Judaizers, who presented themselves as 'super-apostles' (11:5), whereas the Spirit-people could not.

The danger from without represented by the Judaizers was intensified by the hostility of the community to Paul arising out of his refusal to accept their financial support. This had been made to appear as his repudiation of their friendship and as an affront to their self-image (cf. pp. 96–8). As long as the

---

68 'Though Paul is familiar with ecstatic experience as a rare exception, the Spirit, nevertheless, does not mean to him the capacity for mystical experiences. Rather, everything indicates that by the term "Spirit" he means the eschatological existence into which the believer is placed by having appropriated the salvation deed that occurred in Christ' (R. Bultmann, *Theology of the New Testament* (London, 1965), vol. I, 335).

community believed this slander it was vulnerable to Paul's opponents, and so he had to explain his attitude (11:7–11). He had, in fact, done so before (1 Cor. 9:1–18), when his apostolate was attacked on other grounds. Then the argument of his opponents had run as follows: if he does not accept money, it is because he has no right to support; but true apostles do have this right, therefore he cannot be an apostle. Now the angle of attack is different, because what is questioned is not his authority in itself but his relationship to the community. Only when we put the two replies together can we get a clear idea of how Paul understood the relation between ministry and money.

Paul's basic principle is that acceptance of the gospel should not be directly linked to support of the preacher (11:9b); the good news should be given 'free of charge' (1 Cor. 9:18). Such disinterestedness enhanced his credibility, because it showed that he preached out of utter conviction; necessity was laid upon him and he had no choice (1 Cor. 9:16). Moreover, if the gospel is addressed to *all* humanity, it could not in practice be limited to those who could afford to have it proclaimed to them. To select mission areas on the basis of the availability of financial support flatly contradicts the universality of God's message; the poor would not have the gospel preached to them (cf. Matt. 1:5). Finally, Paul was aware of the social convention that the giving and acceptance of a monetary gift established a patron–client relationship. To have accepted support from any community in which he was working would have put him in the position of a client and thus subtly diminished his authority and freedom of movement.

The depth of Paul's conviction in this matter can be gauged from the fact that he consciously put himself in opposition to a directive of Christ: 'The Lord commanded those who proclaim the gospel to get their living from the gospel' (1 Cor. 9:14).[69] This imposes an obligation, yet Paul felt free to ignore it. His arguments outweighed the force of the directive, and this is an extremely important indication of how he interpreted the

---

[69] See D. L. Dungan, *The Sayings of Jesus in the Churches of Paul. The Use of Tradition in the Regulation of Early Church Life* (Philadelphia, 1971).

moral precepts of the Old Testament, and how he intended his own imperatives to be understood. If his 'disobedience' to the dominical command was not a sin, how could it be a 'sin' for him to flout a social convention, whose principal effect was to give more power to the wealthy (11:7)? He uses ironic exaggeration to force the Corinthians to re-evaluate the convention by which they judged him.

By his own account Paul worked as an artisan in each of the communities in which he ministered (1 Thess. 2:9; 2 Thess. 3:8; 1 Cor. 4:12). Luke adds the specification that he was a tent-maker (Acts 18:3). In the two indirect references to his lifestyle, however, Paul exhibits a typically upper-class attitude towards manual labour; it is slavish (1 Cor. 9:19) and demeaning (11:7).[70] Apparently he was not born to his trade, but deliberately chose it as part of his missionary strategy. If it was the only way to ensure his financial independence, he was prepared to accept the social and economic consequences. Socially, he placed himself in the lowest class, which created difficulty of access to certain groups, and which meant that superior members of his community, e.g. the Spirit-people, could look down upon him and be embarrassed for him. Economically, he commited himself to the hardest of lives. An artisan who stayed in one place and developed a regular clientele had to work all day every day and even then barely made ends meet. Each time Paul went to a new town he had to start afresh, and the opposition of his competitors doubled his difficulties. In addition, he had to make time for his preaching. It is not surprising, therefore, that he should often have been 'in want' (11:9), despite the sacrifice of sleep in order to make up time (11:27; 2 Thess. 3:8).

He was fortunate that communities such as Philippi (Phil. 4:15) recognized his straits and sent him money. Otherwise he could not have maintained his principles and survived. It is possible that he was humiliated by such a compromise, but sacrifices had to be made for the sake of the gospel. His description of the aid he received from the Macedonian

[70] R. F. Hock, 'Paul's Tentmaking and the Problem of his Social Class', *JBL* 97 (1978), 555–64.

churches while working in Corinth as 'robbery' (11:8) may be a rhetorical flourish, but it was also a way of signalling to the Corinthians that he had not thereby become a client of the Macedonians. Distance diminished the dangerous aspect of the patron–client relationship.

He had made a bad mistake in not telling the Corinthians the full truth, but neither had he told them an outright lie. He had told them that he had not made '*full* use of my right in the gospel' (1 Cor. 9:18), which is perhaps the earliest Christian example of a mental reservation! He was making *some* use of his right to be supported. Even though he was now at a distance from Corinth, he refused to apply the same principle to the Corinthians. He would not take money from them even if they were the last church on earth (11:9b). His anger at the way his attitude was maliciously misrepresented and at the credence the Corinthians gave such an interpretation is manifest. His hurt is speaking, but he was also deeply saddened that they had failed to perceive the importance of existential witness in the service of the gospel. Their attachment to worldly values and standards remained intact. All he can do is affirm his love for them (11:11). His negative attitude towards the support they offered is motivated by love. He wanted and still desires that they should *see* the power of grace at work in him; it is the only convincing argument of the truth he proclaimed. His choice of a demeaning lifestyle and a precarious existence strips away the veils that cloud conventional vision. They had an opportunity to see him as he is, the embodiment of the 'life of Jesus' (4:10), but were blinded by an expectation based on worldly standards.

The Judaizers, on the contrary, flattered the Corinthians by conforming to their expectations. They felt that their authority was recognized by the financial support they accepted (11:20). In Paul's eyes, however, this vitiated their claim to be authentic 'apostles of Christ' (11:13). He does not dispute that they had the right to support (1 Cor. 9:1–18), but their insistence on this right demonstrates that their interest in the gospel is commercial. They must in consequence be 'false apostles, deceitful workmen and servants of Satan' (11:13–14). This extremely harsh assessment is probably unfair to the intentions of the Judaizers, and is motivated less by the truth of their attitude than by Paul's conviction that the power of the gospel must be manifest in the lives of those who preach it. Those who for the sake of popularity or a sympathetic hearing accept the standards of the world compromise their ministry, and do more harm than good. It is not inappropriate for Paul to judge others by the high standard he sets for himself based on his understanding of the ministry of Jesus Christ (5:15; 8:9).

If Paul excoriates the Judaizers, he is no less hard on the community, whose gullibility he ridicules with unrestrained irony. They should understand his 'foolishness' (the boasting he is going to indulge in) perfectly because they love 'fools' (11:16, 19). In context, this can only be a reference to the Judaizers. The Corinthians are so 'wise' that they let the fools walk all over them (11:20). They like it when someone lords it over them, and willingly embrace slavery. They permit intruders to eat them out of house and home. They love to be taken in. They have so little self-respect that they just put up with it when they are struck in the face. Again there is an element of rhetorical exaggeration, but Paul is deadly serious in his concern to bring home to the Corinthians that they have been duped by the Judaizers, at least on the social level. But it was precisely this that constituted a grave danger on the theological level (11:3). If they had proved receptive to the presence of the Judaizers, they might also welcome their ideas, and this is what Paul really feared (11:4).

It is touching that in the middle of this tirade, in which anxiety fuels anger, Paul's scruples appear (11:16–18). He is aware that his savage attack on all at Corinth is, like his boasting, 'according to the flesh' and not 'according to the Lord'. In order to get through to the Corinthians he has adopted the standards of the world; he finds himself conduct-ing 'a fleshly war' (10:3). His bitter invective is more suited to a politician than to a pastor. In striving to attain a good end he has adopted tainted means. This is his real 'foolish-ness', yet wretchedly he ploughs ahead, talking like a madman (11:23).

FOOLISH BOASTING (11:21B–12:13)

Since Paul was forced into this humiliating position (12:11), we can be sure that what he boasts about was indicated by the claims of the Judaizers. His plan is to match boast with boast; to go any further would be even more unjustifiable. So we can infer that they extolled their Jewishness, their accomplishments and their visions and revelations.

Paul has little difficulty with the first point. He too is a Jew ('Israelite'), of Aramaic-speaking stock ('Hebrew'; cf. Phil. 3:5),[71] and as far as it can be traced back his lineage is Jewish ('seed of Abraham') (11:12). Culturally, racially and religiously he is no whit inferior to his opponents.

According to Greek rhetorical convention concerning comparison, breeding is followed by accomplishments. His adversaries claim to be 'servants of Christ'; he can make the same boast (11:23a; cf. 11:13), and it is much more fully verified in his case. Were Paul boasting seriously he would have listed the number of communities which he had founded, and the wide range of converts he had made. He does touch on this aspect, but only indirectly and at the very end (11:28). With ruthless irony he turns the convention upside down and parodies the self-display of his opponents by highlighting what he should hide and minimizing what should be accentuated.[72] This, however, is not cleverness for its own sake. Paul is still trying to inculcate an understanding of ministry radically different from that proposed by his opponents and desired by the Corinthians.

His apostolic labours have often brought him to the point of death (11:23). One could starve in prison, and the floggings inflicted by Jewish (five times) and Roman authorities (three times) were as little concerned with the survival of the victim as the mob who pelted him with stones. Here Paul graphically illustrated what he means by 'bearing in the body the dying of

---

[71] See W. Gutbrod, 'Hebraios', *TDNT*, 3, 388–91; and J. A. Fitzmyer, *Paul and His Theology. A Brief Sketch* (Englewood Cliffs, NJ, 1989), 9 = *NJBC* 79 (1989), 15.

[72] Forbes, 'Comparison', 18–21.

Jesus', which is the means whereby 'the life of Jesus' is manifested (4:10–11).

His travels were equally fraught with danger;[73] accidents and natural disasters put him at risk. Neither was he safe on the road or in the towns and villages through which he passed. The Roman empire was not well policed. Bandits infested the countryside, and the towns and villages exhibited the anarchy that characterized cow towns in the American west before the establishment of law and order. Paul was always the outsider who could be victimized at will (11:26). The strain which this imposed on him was compounded by the pressure inherent in paying his way and earning a living (11:27), and by his anxiety for all the communities for which he was responsible (11:28). Communications were difficult and slow, and churches might be subjected to persecution or might be following a false line of theological development without his knowing it. Through no fault of his own, the help they needed from him was not always available, but with the unreasonableness which betrays authentic love he felt that he should be at their side in moments of difficulty.

Paul's description of himself as 'weak' (11:29) is the inevitable outcome of his experience of the reality of the human condition. Again and again it was impressed on him that he was without power, status or security (cf. 1 Cor. 9:22). His converts also were for the most part marginalized (1 Cor. 1:26–7), as were the majority of those to whom he preached. He knew what was going on in their lives because he was subject to the same alienating pressures. Despite his idealistic commitment to Christ, he must have been continuously beset by the temptation of selfishness. In order to survive he had to compete for work, and he had to ensure that his precious wallet of tools (awl, needles, waxed thread) was not stolen. This led him to see those to whom his ministry was directed as victimized by the false value system of society which imposed on them an egocentric mode of existence. If they did not look out for themselves, no one else would. Society imposed on them a lifestyle which was the antithesis of the way God, as revealed

73 See my 'On the Road and on the Sea with St. Paul', *Bible Review* 1, 2 (1985), 38–47.

in Christ (5:15), desired human beings to live. It is here that we see the origins of the concept of Sin as a controlling force which plays such a major role in Romans (Rom. 3:9; 5:12; 6:6, 14, 17, 20, 23; 7:14, 23). Naturally, he burns with anger when they are 'humiliated' (11:29). He is thinking not merely of the casual contempt of the upper class, but of the brutalizing effect of social forces which make them untrue to themselves.

Paul concludes his list of 'accomplishments' with a graphic account of his humiliating escape from Damascus (11:32-3). He had already spoken of his ministry as the seige of an enemy city (10:3-6), and one of the highest Roman military awards for valour was the 'wall crown' (shaped to represent a turreted wall) accorded to the first centurion up and over a defended city wall. Such an exploit is derisively parodied in Paul's picture of his descent of the wall like a helpless baby in a basket.[74]

A very different version of this episode is given by Luke in Acts 9:23-5, who mistakenly assumed the threat to come from the Jews. If Paul had got into trouble in Arabia and had had to flee to Damascus for safety (Gal. 1:17), it would explain why the Nabataeans, whose king was Aretas IV (9 BC–AD 40), wanted to apprehend him. Only after the death of the emperor Tiberius on 16 March AD 37 could they have resumed control of Damascus, because it was his successor Gaius (AD 37–41) who reinstated the policy of client kingdoms on the eastern frontier, and he had reasons to be well disposed to the Nabataeans. Thus Paul's escape from Damascus and his first visit to Jerusalem as a Christian (Gal. 1:18) can be dated in the years AD 37–9, with the probability that it was earlier in this period rather than later.[75]

Once again underlining the pointlessness of boasting, Paul turns to the question of visions and revelations, on which his

---

[74] See E. A. Judge, 'Paul's Boasting in Relation to Contemporary Professional Practice', *AusBR* 16 (1968), 47.

[75] G. Lüdemann's attempt to dismiss this argument (*Paul, Apostle to the Gentiles. Studies in Chronology* (London, 1984), 31, note 10) has been convincingly countered by R. Jewett (*Dating Paul's Life* (London, 1979), 30-3), but what the latter takes from Josephus has to be revised in the light of C. Saulnier, 'Hérode Antipas et Jean le Baptiste. Quelques Remarques sur les confusions chronologiques de Flavius Josephe', *RB* 91 (1984), 362–76.

opponents laid such emphasis (12:1). It is neither a proof of
authentic ministry nor beneficial to the community. Unless
one is prepared to lie or to embroider wildly, it is extremely
difficult to speak ironically about such experiences. Paul gets
around the difficulty very neatly by writing of himself in the
third person (12:2–5), thereby distancing himself from the
episode. The function of the date ('fourteen years ago' = AD 41)
is to underline the reality of the experience. God carried him up
to the third heaven,[76] which, in keeping with one strand of
Jewish cosmology, he identifies as Paradise (2 Enoch 7;
Apocalypse of Moses 37:5), but he cannot say how he got there
nor divulge what he heard. By attributing it to someone else
Paul underlines the irrelevance of the experience for his
ministry. It did not change him in any way and it did not
furnish him with any information which he could use. The
unstated critique of his opponents is obvious. If their experience was the same as Paul's, it contributed nothing. If their
experience was something they could talk about, it was less
ineffable than his.

Even though he had plenty which he could truthfully boast
about, Paul wants to be judged not on what he might say about
himself, but on his comportment and preaching (12:6). The
only true test of a minister is the extent to which he manifests
'the life of Jesus' in his behaviour (4:10–11) and effectively
proclaims the saving death of Christ (5:15). Paul is aware that
he did neither perfectly (Phil. 3:12–16), and does not want to
be reputed above his achievements, particularly since God has
ensured that he does not estimate himself too highly (12:7).

In order to keep Paul humble and to ensure that he did not
forget his weaknesses, God had given him 'a thorn in the flesh,
a messenger of Satan' (12:7). Over the centuries a great
number of suggestions have been made as to what this is.[77]

---

[76] A journey to another world is a common theme in apocalyptic literature, see A. F.
Segal, 'Heavenly Ascent in Hellenistic Judaism, Early Christianity and Their
Environment', *ANRW* 2, 23/2, 1333–94.

[77] V. P. Furnish offers a good survey of the proposals, but opts for some type of illness
(*II Corinthians* (AB; Garden City, NY, 1984), 548–50). The position adopted here
has been well argued by T. Y. Mullins, 'Paul's Thorn in the Flesh', *JBL* 76 (1957),
299–303.

Some identify it as a bodily ailment, e.g. a speech impediment, epilepsy, malaria, bad eyesight, etc. Whereas others think in terms of a mental illness such as a tendency to depression. Such speculation, however, has little if anything to justify it. The two phrases 'thorn in the flesh' and 'messenger of Satan' are not causally connected but stand in apposition, which suggests an external personal source of affliction. This interpretation is confirmed by the use of 'thorns' in the Old Testament to mean enemies (e.g. Num. 33:55; Ezek. 28:24), and by Paul's identification of his opponents as 'servants of Satan' (11:14–15). The point would seem to be that there was always someone in his communities who gave him grief, so that Paul could never rest on his laurels. He could never sit back and complacently contemplate a perfect community. There was always maintenance work to be done, and this must have been extremely irritating to Paul, whose gift was to found new churches and whose ambition was to reach out into ever new territory.

It is not surprising that he prayed regularly to be released from this affliction (12:8). The response he received is couched in the form of a divine oracle (12:9). This does not mean that Paul was conscious of a heavenly voice speaking within his mind. The form simply emphasizes the importance which he attaches to the insight. By what mode of reflection he reached this conclusion we can never know, but he held it with utter conviction as the expression of God's will for him. The perfect tense 'he has said' indicates a permanently valid decision; there will be no more prayers for release.

A literal translation of the oracle brings out its concentric structure, which is an important clue to its meaning 'It suffices [A] for you [B] my grace [C] for this power [C'] in weakness [B'] is perfected [A']' (12:9a).[78] Clearly the second part is not a generic principle; it clarifies the first part which applies specifically to Paul. Thus 'weakness' is the condition of being subject to 'insults, hardships, persecutions, difficulties'

---

[78] G. O'Collins, 'Power made Perfect in Weakness: 2 Cor. 12:9–10', *CBQ* 33 (1971), 528–37, here 534.

(12:10). Paul does not seek out such suffering.[79] As any normal person, he struggles against it, but has finally come to realize that he is as nothing when measured against the force of a false value system firmly rooted in the institutions of a great society. Any effort to change this world, which is what his mission demands, necessarily brings him into conflict with entrenched positions. In worldly terms, he is powerless, devoid of the leverage given by wealth, position or birth, and the chance of success is negligible.

Yet he has achieved something: believing communities do exist, and individuals have committed themselves to a new vision, whatever inadequacies there may be in its practical realization. The grace of God is sufficient; the power of Christ is real because it has effected change. When he was at Corinth 'in weakness, and in much fear and trembling' his ministry was endowed with 'the Spirit and power' (1 Cor. 2:3–4), and the result is Corinthian Christians (1 Cor. 9:2; 2 Cor. 3:2). This is the paradox: 'when I am weak then I am strong' (12:10). There is a radical disproportion between what he *is* and what he *does*.

What precisely is the relationship between 'weakness' and 'power' in Paul's mind? In saying 'I will all the more gladly boast of my weaknesses in order that the power of Christ may reside with me' (12:9b), he gives the impression that 'weakness' is the precondition for the reception of God's gracious power,[80] and seems to imply that one is proportionate to the other; the greater the weakness the greater the power. It is very unlikely that Paul intended to be understood in this way. 'Weakness' in this context must be interpreted socially, not psychologically. It does not connote a sense of inadequacy before God or a posture of self-abasement. It evokes the condition of being without anything that in the eyes of the world would make his mission feasible, together with the concomitant mental and physical suffering. This is not a

---

[79] According to J. Dunn, 'Paul's attitude towards suffering is nothing if not positive. He does not merely endure it in stoical fashion. He welcomes it and rejoices in it' (*Jesus and the Spirit. A Study of the Religious and Charismatic Experience of Jesus and the First Christians as Reflected in the New Testament* (Philadelphia, 1975), 327). This is contradicted by 12:8, where he prays that suffering might leave him.

[80] See for example, Dunn, *Jesus and the Spirit*, 329.

lifestyle which Paul has chosen, a conscious emptying in order
to be filled with the power of Christ. His fundamental decision
is to follow Christ as an apostle, and it has been borne in upon
him progressively that this involves 'bearing in his body the
dying of Jesus' (4:10). His suffering is not willed directly,
which would be perverse, but is accepted as a necessary
consequence. Inevitably, therefore, he sees 'weakness' as the
concrete modality in which his ministry is lived out. In reality,
to boast of his weaknesses is to express his pride in the ministry
entrusted to him, and it is his commitment to this ministry
which gives him a claim to the power of Christ.

The shift from 'the grace of God' (12:9) to 'the power of
Christ' (12:10) underlines the strong Christological orientation
of Paul's concept of ministry. God's saving grace was first
manifested in history in the person of Christ: 'the power of God
and the wisdom of God' (1 Cor. 1:24). During Christ's lifetime,
however, what was apparent was his 'weakness' (8:9; 13:4),
but now he lives by the power of God (13:4) and his ministry is
prolonged in the lives of those who in their comportment
exhibit both 'the dying of Jesus' and 'the life of Jesus'
(4:10–11). The continuity is underlined by the simultaneity of
weakness and power.

The intrinsic relationship between ministry and grace (the
former is impossible without the latter) does not exclude
another aspect of 'weakness'. The discrepancy between what
Paul is and what he achieves reveals that the power at his
disposal is of divine origin (4:7). This power is that of the cross
of Christ (1 Cor. 1:17), which a minister may nullify by failing
to live in imitation of Christ (5:15) or by trying to make the
gospel attractive by adapting it to the standards of the world
(1 Cor. 1:17; 2:1–5). But by permitting himself to be transformed by grace from glory to glory into the image of Christ
(3:18) the divine power acts through him, and its origins are
made manifest in so far as no natural gifts can account for its
effect in the lives of others.

Paul is serious in boasting about his weaknesses, but he is
still highly embarrassed. Boasting is designed to attract credit
to oneself, but what the minister accomplishes is due to grace,

and so all praise should go to the Lord (10:17; cf. 1 Cor. 1:31). Thus, once again he proclaims himself a fool (12:11), and offers a justification similar to that contained in the introduction to the Fool's Speech (11:1–21a). He is forced to speak about himself because the Corinthians have failed to do so (12:11b). They should have praised him in response to the slanderous criticism of his opponents, because they knew (1 Cor. 9:2) that he is no whit inferior to those who considered themselves super-apostles (cf. 11:5). Despite his unimpressive presence and poor speech (10:10), they had experienced the power of his ministry in their lives. They were perfectly aware that he was much more than the 'nothing' his adversaries claimed he was (12:11c). Paul's irony has become much gentler, perhaps because the gibe has reminded him of what he had previously written to the Corinthians: 'Without love I am nothing' (1 Cor. 13:2). His love for them (2:4; 8:7; 11:11; 12:15) stands in vivid contrast to the way they were exploited by the intruders (11:20). He has repeatedly suggested that his opponents were inspired by self-interest, whereas he is motivated by the love of Christ (5:14). In this sense, therefore, his adversaries were 'nothing'.

With an abruptness that is rather surprising, Paul goes on to discuss 'the signs of an apostle' (12:12). It seems likely that this formula stems from the Corinthians. The Judaizers had tried to replace the authority of Paul by their own, and the community was forced into the position of having to choose between them and their significantly different gospels. It was natural that the church should look for a standard against which each could be measured. In their world it was widely believed that explicit and unambiguous manifestations of divine power were the concomitant and guarantee of authentic religious truth. Thus miracles became the criterion.

Paul does not agree that this is a valid standard. Not only is Christ the sole criterion (4:10–11; 5:15–17), but the ability to work miracles is a spiritual gift which must be distinguished from the gift of apostleship (1 Cor. 12:29–30). None the less, the object of this 'foolishness' (11:1, 16; 12:11) is to beat his opponents on their own ground, however irrelevant their criteria might be. Hence, he has to say something about 'signs and wonders and mighty works' (12:12). No more than in other letters does he claim to have worked miracles (cf. Rom. 15:19; Gal. 3:5; 1 Cor. 2:4). What he did was to 'endure' the slights and sufferings which were the consequences of his 'weakness'. It was God who performed the miraculous signs which graced his ministry. These were not given to enhance the stature of Paul but, as he underlines with biting irony, for the sake of the community: 'In what were you less favoured than other churches?' (12:13a). In Paul's eyes such extraordinary events were of much less significance than the power of the gospel (Rom. 1:16), whose effect is to transform lives.

This perspective on Paul's ministry, in which miracles appear to be no more than an unnecessary by-product, contrasts vividly with that of Luke. He depicts Paul and Barnabas as reporting with pride to the Jerusalem conference on 'the signs and wonders God had done through them among the gentiles' (Acts 15:12), and records miracles of Paul at Paphos (Acts 13:11), at Iconium (Acts 14:3), at Lystra (Acts 14:8), at Philippi (Acts 16:16–18), at Ephesus (Acts 19:11–12), at Troas (Acts 20:10) and on Malta (Acts 28:1–9). The only notable exceptions are Galatia, Thessalonica and Corinth, but his silence regarding these cities is certainly due to the inadequacy of his sources, because for each Paul himself notes the occurrence of miracles (Gal. 3:5; 1 Thess. 1:5; 1 Cor. 2:4; 2 Cor. 12:12).

The differing attitudes of Luke and Paul towards the latter's miracles highlights how unique Paul was. Luke accepted the conventions of his age and found witness value in Paul's quality as a wonder-worker. Paul is much more sensitive to what is new in Christianity. For him the essential is to be conformed to Christ (Rom. 8:29) in such a way as to project the reality of a new authentic humanity (1 Cor. 11:1). This existential gospel is *the* miracle of the eschaton, which must be multiplied throughout all humanity. To display thus the power of grace is not the prerogative of Paul alone, but the responsibility of all who in baptism have put on Christ (Gal. 3:27) and are committed to 'holding forth the word of life' (Phil. 2:16).

The new form of God's action in history, which makes Christianity unique, is a creative love which breaks the bonds of Sin and both enables and inspires others 'to live no longer for themselves but for him who for their sake died and was raised' (5:15).

While recognizing healings and exorcisms as manifestations of divine power, his reticence indicates that Paul sees their sign value as much more ambiguous than behaviour exhibiting 'the life of Jesus' (4:10–11). With a little organization, such miracles are easily faked, and the religious charlatans of his day did so regularly and extremely effectively. Even when they are authentic, these miracles paradoxically deflect attention from God and his plan to bring into being a 'new creation' (5:17). The wonder-workers are immediately accessible and can be approached in a more satisfying direct way. They are adulated and held in high regard; but they are also feared because they might withhold their power, and so are placated by gifts and obedience. It is easy to see how this could lead to a form of authority and a modality of religious leadership which for Paul was the antithesis of what is needed to form an authentic community. Instead of representing the ideal towards which the members strive, such leaders would tend to lord it over them, rather than offer them the service of love (1:24; 4:5).

If miracles are given undue prominence, there are also consequences for the community. The members tend to think that divine gifts should take dramatic forms or to expect God to intervene directly in response to their prayers. Without excluding either, Paul none the less believes that grace is normally given in the interaction of Christians who respond to one another with the multiple manifestations of genuine love (1 Cor. 13:1–13; Gal. 5:22; Rom. 12:9–13). Miracles may astound and reassure, but the manifestations of divine power which are necessary for the following of Christ are such gifts as inspiration, encouragement, consolation, understanding and gentleness.

CHAPTER 10

A warning prepares a visit (12:14–13:13)

From the beginning Paul knew that Letter B could not solve the problems at Corinth. The news from Corinth had taken a minimum of two weeks to reach him in western Macedonia or Illyricum, which meant that his response would be at least four weeks out of date by the time it arrived in Corinth. The situation there was extremely volatile, and the circumstances of the community might have changed to the point that his letter might be at best irrelevant or at worst dangerous, since words written for one situation may acquire a different meaning in altered circumstances.

Once before he had substituted a letter for a visit (2:1–4), and the result had been most satisfactory (7:5–16) – or so he thought at the time. Now he knows that there were under-currents whose significance had gone unremarked, and that he cannot postpone a visit (10:2, 11). Equally, however, he cannot simply abandon the new communities he is building up in the virgin territory west of Beroea. Their fragility has a claim on his nurturing care. He needs time to disengage himself gently from these new converts. Thus he writes Letter B to the Corinthians as a stop-gap, whose main objective is to prevent things getting completely out of hand at Corinth. It is obvious that the effect of the letter will have an impact on the sort of reception which awaits Paul at Corinth. Hence, he brings the issue into the open. The hints of 10:2 and 11 are clarified in a formal promise; he is actively preparing to come to Corinth (12:14; 13:1–2).[81]

---

[81] In itself, 2 Corinthians 12:14 is ambiguous because 'as far as grammar is concerned *triton touto* may be taken with either *hetoimos echo* or *elthein*' (A. Plummer, *A Critical and*

The extent to which the slanders regarding his attitude towards money weigh on Paul's mind is emphasized by the fact that he returns to this topic, even though he has dealt with it at length in 11:7–11. His concern is to dispel the miasma of suspicion that has poisoned the atmosphere. But he will not compromise his principle. He will not 'burden' them (12:14a) by accepting their support (cf. 11:9b). Not only does he have good reasons for his position which are rooted in his understanding of witness, but to give in at precisely this juncture would mean the end of his authority at Corinth. He would be putting himself in the position of a client subject to the whims of his patron, and thus abrogating the responsibility his ministry placed upon him. A client could not challenge or correct his patron, and a pastor still had much to do in both those areas at Corinth (cf. 12:19–21).

Paul is obviously much less tense and heated than in his tirade in 11:7–11, and he finds new reasons to justify his attitude. The lapidary formula 'I seek not what is yours but you' (12:14a), which may have been suggested by the behaviour of his opponents (11:20), perfectly expresses his perspectives on ministry. His sole goal is to win all for Christ, not to enrich himself or to enhance his authority. He is nothing more than an instrument in God's hands (1 Cor. 3:5), and his only motive is the implementation of God's plan for the transformation of humanity.

He makes his meaning clear with a very homely example (12:14b). The Corinthians had not disputed his claim to be their spiritual father (11:2; cf. 1 Cor. 4:14–15), and they must know that it is parents who provide for their children and not the other way around. It is he who must give to them and not

Exegetical Commentary on the Second Epistle of St Paul to the Corinthians (ICC; Edinburgh, 1915), 361). In consequence, there are two possible translations: (1) 'This is the third time I am making preparations to come to you'; and (2) 'This is the third visit which I am preparing to pay you.' The implication of (1) is that Paul had not visited Corinth since he founded the church there; he had made a number of attempts to return but had never succeeded. The implication of (2) is that Paul had already visited Corinth twice, when he founded the church and on a subsequent occasion, the so-called intermediate visit. Interpretation (1) is defended by N. Hyldahl ('Die Frage nach der literarischen Einheit des Zweiten Korintherbriefes', *ZNW* 64 (1973), 303–4), but interpretation (2) is demanded by 2 Corinthians 13:1–2.

they to him, and he is willing to give his all on their behalf
(12:15a). He cannot provide for them financially, but he does
pour out on them the manifold gifts of love, through which
passes the grace which makes and maintains their new being in
Christ. Should not they in turn respond with love and trust
(6:11–13)? Is the more love he shows them a reason for their
loving him less (12:15b)? The irony is pathetic in its delicacy.
Humanly, he yearns for their affection, but there is more to it
than that. The test of authentic Christianity is loving (1 Cor.
13:2), and Paul sees the Corinthians' attitude towards him as
indicative of a failure to appreciate the ideal which he has set
before them. Their willingness to misinterpret his motives in
refusing assistance is a sign that they have not really accepted
the standard of human behaviour set by Christ (5:15). They
should trust and try to understand. Instead they have put their
faith in a social convention which is essentially a means of
manipulation and control. They persist in judging by worldly
criteria.

The extent to which the Corinthians are dominated by
worldly attitudes appears most clearly in the charge which
Paul now repeats, 'He did not ask us for money for himself, but
like a confidence trickster he used deceit to take us in' (12:16).
The reference to Titus and the brother (12:18) indicates that
the allegation of dishonesty concerns the collection for the poor
of Jerusalem (8:23). It must have been suggested that Paul
could afford to spurn Corinthian support because he and/or
his agents were dipping into the funds collected for Jerusalem.
Both the depth of malice behind the accusation, and the
animosity towards Paul which made it palatable at Corinth,
become clear once it is recalled that the Corinthians were
perfectly aware of the precautions which Paul had taken to
ensure that nothing like this could possibly happen (8:20). At
Corinth each was to present his or her accumulated savings on
the collection day, when the total sum would be carried to
Jerusalem by their own elected representatives (1 Cor.
16:1–14). A delegate selected by the churches of Macedonia to
oversee the collection at Corinth was a further guarantee
(8:18–19). In fairness, the Corinthians should have assumed

that Paul had made the same careful arrangements elsewhere, particularly since he had as good as told them that the Macedonians were free to make their own decision as to how to get their contribution to Jerusalem; they might or might not travel with him (9:4).

Paul has every reason to feel deeply hurt at the currency given such a demonstrably false and ugly slander, and must have thought deeply about the reception he was likely to receive at Corinth. He could have pleaded for the simple justice of a fair hearing, but with grim dignity he coldly demands that they specify the charges (12:18). Where, when and how did either he or Titus defraud them? Can they truly say that both he and Titus ever acted with less than perfect integrity? There is no more to be said. The answers will have to await his arrival at Corinth.

The propensity of the Corinthians to believe the worst of him diverts Paul's thought into another channel. Their lack of any moral standard in his regard reminds him of other moral failings which have been brought to his attention. To deal with them he has to reassert his authority as pastor. Much of what he had written in Letter B could give the impression that he and the Judaizers were competing for the favour of the Corinthians. The intruders made claims and he topped them. However, by his repeated characterization of this procedure as 'foolishness' (11:1, 16, 21, 23; 12:11) Paul has indicated that he was not taking this silly game seriously, and evidently hoped that the Corinthians would understand what he was trying to achieve. None the less, he had few illusions about their ability to misunderstand him (1:13), and so he brings out into the open what he presumes their interpretation is, namely, that he has been defending himself before them (12:19a), as if his primary concern were his own reputation and his good standing in the community.

In reply, Paul insists that he has simply been using rather novel means to get across to them what authentic ministry is and how it achieves its goal (12:19b; cf. 2:17). He speaks 'before God', because it is God who has chosen and empowered him, and who will be his final judge (1 Cor. 4:1–4).

He speaks 'in Christ' because as a Christian he demonstrates the present reality of grace by exhibiting in his comportment 'the life of Jesus' (4:10–11). Without which existential reinforcement his proclamation of the meaning of the death of Christ (5:15) might appear as mere fantasy. This in itself, without any reference to the concomitant sufferings, guarantees that he has not been acting for his own benefit. Everything that he says and does is dedicated to the 'upbuilding' of the Corinthians. The sole objective of his ministry is to raise them from the existential 'death' of the egocentricity imposed on them by the false value system of society to a new 'life' characterized by the altruism of Christ. It is very significant that just at this point Paul addresses the Corinthians as 'beloved' for the first time in Letter B (cf. 7:1), because it summarizes his repeated affirmations of his love for them (11:2; 11; 12:15). This love, rooted in that of Christ (5:14), is the concrete modality of the creative force of grace which enables them to change.

In theory, this change from 'death' to 'life' is accomplished at the moment when commitment to Christ is socially ratified by submission to the ritual of baptism (Gal. 3:26–8), but Paul was fully aware of the time-lag between an intellectual decision and the realization of a radically new lifestyle. His converts were adults and the self-centred habits acquired over many years did not disappear automatically: they had to be eradicated by continuous conscious striving towards the ideal represented by Christ, and 'the desires of the flesh' did not give way easily to 'the desires of the Spirit' (Gal. 5:13–25).

Thus in all his communities Paul had to undertake a programme of moral re-education. His procedure was to make a minimum number of suggestions (e.g. 1 Thess. 4:1–8) and then let the believers work things out for themselves (Phil. 1:9–10; Col. 1:9–10). It was their responsibility to discern the truth, and this meant that he had to allow them the freedom to make mistakes. The Corinthians took full advantage of this liberty, and 1 Corinthians offers a perfect illustration of how Paul handled such problems. He never authoritatively imposes a solution, but outlines the theological and Christological principles involved, and then indicates what he would do in the circumstances (e.g. 1 Cor. 8:1–13). It was then up to the Corinthians to rethink their position and to find a more authentic way of expressing their Christianity socially.

In view of the crisis which had developed at Corinth subsequent to the writing of 1 Corinthians, Paul had good reason to think that issues of practical Christian living had been pushed into the background. It was both more exciting and less demanding to debate the qualities of different leaders and the merits of different forms of Christianity. As such discussions became more passionate there was the eminent likelihood of 'quarrelling, jealousy, anger, intrigues, slander, gossip, conceit, and disorder' (12:20). This possibility makes Paul 'afraid' because such attitudes are indicative of a complete breakdown of trust, co-operation and mutual support, which are the conditions that make a community a vital source of divine grace.[82] He would be forced to take severe action because in his view divisions and their consequences were characteristic of society (Gal. 3:28; 5:19–21; Rom. 1:29–31; 1 Cor. 5:10–11; 6:9–10). He could not permit a grouping that was only nominally different from those in the world to continue masquerading as a Christian community. That would be to perpetuate a living lie and to constitute a sign contrary to the gospel.

Paul's second fear is that God will humiliate him once again (12:21a). He probably has in mind the hostile reception he got during his second visit, when the Corinthians did not accept his authority and adopted a neutral stance when he was insulted (2:1–11). To be ignored by his own converts must have been intensely humiliating, and his failure to retaliate was interpreted as cowardice (10:1b). It is typical of Paul's theological stance that he should make God responsible for such humiliation. His belief in the universal efficacy of God's will is so strong that he is convinced that the Corinthians could have

---

[82] So, rightly, Furnish (*II Corinthians*, 567), but he does not adequately emphasize that the correlation of the sins mentioned in the next verse (12:21) with those condemned in 1 Corinthians indicates that Paul is thinking of a particular section of the community.

acted as they did only with divine approbation. Paul is human enough not to desire a repetition of the experience, but in the mystery of God's plan it might have an unforeseen role to play in both his conformation to Christ (12:7–10) and that of the community. As this letter shows, however, Paul does not understand such humiliation as punishment for his inadequacies or as a sign that he is on the wrong track. The fact that its meaning escapes him does not cloud his vision of the goal of his ministry or exempt him from continuing effort to form Christ in those entrusted to his charge.

Concern for the basic structure of the community and his own position within it do not exhaust Paul's fears. In 1 Corinthians he had to draw the attention of the Corinthians to the destructive impact of incest on the community's witness (1 Cor. 5:1–5) and to the selfishness intrinsic to the frequentation of prostitutes (1 Cor. 6:12–20). The Spirit-people, who denied the moral relevance of all corporeal actions (1 Cor. 6:18b), were certainly at fault in the latter instance, and undoubtedly were among those who approved of incest as a sign of their total liberty. Knowing their opposition to his leadership, Paul had reasons to think it probable that they might have ignored his corrective suggestions. Hence, he once again warns 'those who sinned before' to repent of their 'uncleanness, fornication, and flagrant public immorality' (12:21b).

Having issued these formal warnings to those guilty of sexual sins and to the rest who were drawn into the factions within the community, Paul solemnly draws their attention to the fact that this is the second formal admonition that they have received; the first had been given on the occasion of his second visit (13:2).[83] Thus he has scrupulously observed the rule laid down in Deuteronomy 19:15 (13:16), which in Palestinian Judaism was interpreted to mean that wrong-doers had to be warned two or three times before punishment could

---

[83] The sentence is complex because Paul is thinking in two time-frames. 'I said earlier' goes with 'being present the second time'; in this case 'earlier' (which I use to translate the prefix *pro* – which appears in both verbs) refers to a time before the present (the intermediate visit to Corinth). 'I say earlier' goes with 'being absent now'; in this case 'earlier' evokes the present as contrasted with the future when Paul will be once again at Corinth.

be inflicted.[84] On his imminent third visit, therefore, he will be free to mete out such penalties as he deems appropriate.

But what could Paul really do? He could not excommunicate his opponents, because the authority to do so belonged to the community. His stress on his spiritual presence in 1 Corinthians 5:1–5 is his way of ensuring that his voice was heard in the community assembly, and his advocacy of excommunication as the only appropriate punishment is strong and unambiguous. Yet he is not ordering the community to take such action. Not only would that be contrary to his principles, but 1 Corinthians 5:2 clearly implies that it is the responsibility of the community to purify itself.[85] On that occasion the community adopted the line suggested by Paul. He could not assume that a similar proposal would now win the same support. His adversaries would certainly resist, and if the majority of the community was prepared to believe ill of him in money matters (12:14–18) there was no guarantee that they would rally to his side.

If the community did not respond to his admonitions, the only alternative was for him to declare that the quality of their lives, both individually and collectively, did not conform to the gospel and that they were not in fact Christians. This would be a terrible decision for Paul to take. It would be the end of the church at Corinth, and all the love and effort that he had invested over five years would be thrown away. Yet, if Christ was truly speaking in him (13:3a), he had no option. He must represent the truth at whatever cost to himself or others (13:8). He cannot salvage his own self-respect by refusing to admit failure if the church at Corinth was only a mockery of what an authentic Christian community should be. That would be to compromise the gospel in a way which would do irreparable damage to his mission. He had to be able to point to his foundations as evidence of the power of grace (3:2; 1 Thess. 1:6–8; Phil. 2:16). Such existential witness was the only guarantee of what he proclaimed. Moreover, he knew that

---

[84] See H. van Vliet, *No Single Testimony: A Study on the Adopting of the Law of Deut. 19:15 Par. into the New Testament* (Utrecht, 1958).

[85] See my '1 Corinthians 5:3–5', *RB* 84 (1977), 239–45.

there would be contacts between his various churches. Business brought Chloe's people from Ephesus to Corinth and naturally they visited the community there (1 Cor. 1:11). If Paul even appeared to accept what was going on at Corinth, other churches might feel free to lower their standards, and the challenge of the Christian ideal would be diluted.

Naturally, Paul shrank from such a confrontation, and this made him conscious of a new dimension of his 'weakness'. But he was also aware of this responsibility as an apostle and the 'power' accorded him to fulfil this role. Thus the tension between weakness and power again surfaces (cf. 12:9–10) and he immediately places it in a strongly Christological context: both weakness and power characterize Christ (13:3b–4a). The former is revealed by the cross, the latter by the resurrection; both are essential to his role in God's plan. His death revealed the true meaning of authentic humanity (5:15), and his power as the risen Lord enables others to rise from 'death' to 'life'. That power had been active among the Corinthians. It had freed them from the slavery of Sin and given them the liberty of the Spirit, which is the beginning of the process that conforms them ever more closely to Christ (3:17–18). Now, however, only faint traces of such grace remain, but the Corinthians must remember what had been wrought among them. Paul might appear weak, but his weakness is that of Christ, and concomitant with it is the power of Christ (12:9).[86] 'We shall live with him by the power of God' (13:4b) is resurrection language (1 Cor. 6:14; Rom. 8:11), but Paul is not thinking eschatologically. The qualifying phrase, 'towards you' or 'in relation to you', indicates that he is thinking in terms of the proximate future, when he will be present at Corinth. In colloquial modern terms he will 'rise' to the situation which confronts him there. The Corinthians may think that they have the upper hand, since Paul will face the community alone, but the power of God is with him and they must reckon with the

---

[86] J. Dunn draws attention to the fact that Paul writes 'we are weak in him' when one might have expected 'we are strong in him'; 'the key fact here is that Christ remains the Crucified even though he now lives by the power of God' (*Jesus and the Spirit. A Study of the Religious and Charismatic Experience of Jesus and the First Christians as Reflected in the New Testament* (Philadelphia, 1975), 331).

possibility of its being deployed in a way which would dismay them. His weakness is but a facet of the lived power-laden gospel, whose truth must prevail.

The Corinthians, therefore, should look to themselves. Instead of trying to put Paul to the test they should examine themselves. They profess to be believing Christians, but are they so in reality (13:5)? Do they in fact measure up to the standard revealed in Christ (5:15)? By starting with their verbal profession of Christianity, Paul neatly reduces to irrelevance whatever they may have considered to be the appropriate manifestations of genuine religiosity. They will be assessed in terms of what they profess.

The ideal which Paul holds up to them is the standard by which he and his collaborators (12:18) will also be judged. He hopes that the Corinthians will have the sincerity to recognize that he strove continuously to be worthy of the gospel he proclaims (13:6). In him they should have caught a glimpse of the criterion against which all believers will be measured (4:10–11; 1 Cor. 11:1).

Having placed himself together with the Corinthians firmly in the shadow of the cross, Paul now abnegates himself even further. What people think of him is irrelevant; they are free to consider him unqualified or a failure; what matters is the quality of life of the community. The Corinthians, therefore, must avoid evil and do good (13:7; cf. 1 Thess. 5:21–2). The Greek word here translated by 'good' is *kalos*, which also carries the connotation of 'noble' and 'beautiful'. Thus something more is meant than actions that are morally irreproachable. Believers must live in a way that commands respect and admiration. Their comportment must exhibit the nobility of true beauty that exercises an attractive force on those who perceive it. It is typical of Paul that he should see the community in missionary terms. It does not exist in and for itself but is destined to shine as a light in the world (Phil. 2:16).

This is the 'truth', the lived gospel, to which Paul's ministry is dedicated (13:8). In his mind there is no distinction between being an apostle and being a believer. Through God's choice, his apostolate is his way of being a Christian (1:1). This is why he cannot 'do anything against the truth'; he would destroy himself in the process, i.e. become a completely different kind of person. Equally, he cannot countenance a 'truth' other than that revealed in Jesus Christ. He cannot accept 'another gospel' (11:4) such as that of the Judaizers, in which Jesus is relegated to insignificance. Nor can he tolerate the Spirit-people's vision of Christianity as a cerebral commitment which has no need of translation into creative mutual love. As Jesus is the truth of Christ (Eph. 4:21), the truth of the gospel is the body of Christ, a community that displays to the world the beauty of grace in action. This is why the 'restoration' of the Corinthians is so important (13:9). They must become in practice what they are in theory (cf. 1 Cor. 5:7–8). It is his concern for this truth which will make him take punitive action when he comes to Corinth unless the situation there has significantly improved (13:10).

In the concluding paragraph of the letter Paul synthesizes his appeal in the simplest possible terms, and in such a way as to underline the community's responsibility for itself. He cannot restore them; they must restore themselves. Were he to force them, their goodness would be by compulsion and not of their own free will (Philem. 14). By acting as a channel of grace he can only make it possible for them to choose a Christ-like mode of being. The choice, however, must be made by them in perfect freedom, otherwise it is meaningless. Thus it is they who must 'admonish one another'. They have a ministry to each other. Paul is not thinking primarily of verbal correction but of a lifestyle modelled on that of Christ (5:15) which is both a challenge and an inspiration to other members of the community. This concretization of the ideal towards which all theoretically strive should focus their attention on what is essential in the gospel and lead to 'agreement' and 'peace'. Fundamentally, he is asking them 'to put on love which binds everything together in perfect harmony' (Col. 3:14). Only then will God truly dwell among them because the sign of his presence is love and peace, which he communicates to those whose hearts are open (13:11). The initial symbol of such openness is the 'holy kiss' which the Corinthians should give one another when they hear this letter read in the public assembly of the community (13:12). It reaffirms the bond of unity which has been shredded by the vicious factionalism (12:20) which Paul hopes will be a thing of the past by the time he arrives. The greeting from the Christians in Macedonia and Illyricum (13:13) reminds them that this bond must include others outside Corinth, the churches from which they have received (1 Thess. 1:7) and to which they owe love.

In the final benediction, which is trinitarian in form but not in substance, Paul formulates both the goal of the letter and the means whereby it is to be achieved (13:14). What he desires above all is that the Corinthians be a 'common union of the Spirit'. The genitive should be given its widest latitude because its basic function is to distinguish the Christian community from secular groupings. The latter are essentially functional associations whose members come together to achieve something beyond the individual capacity of each. They are bound together by a common interest. The members of a believing community, on the contrary, share a common life because they belong to a community of being. Paul uses the image of the body (1 Cor. 12:12–28) to underline that the unity of the community is organic. The members are different because each has a specific gift of the Spirit (1 Cor. 12–14) just as the head, feet and hands are different. Yet these are what they are because they belong to a body. Similarly the diversity of believers is founded in the unity of their being; they share a common existence. They are what they are because they belong to Christ (1 Cor. 3:23). This radically new mode of existence is what Paul means by Spirit, as 'to be in the Spirit' and 'to walk according to the Spirit' indicate.

This new possibility of being is opened to humanity by the love of God which is made present in history through Jesus Christ (Rom. 5:8–9). In him the wisdom of God became visible and his power experienced (1 Cor. 1:24). Both facets of Christ's ministry are represented in that of Paul, who exhibits 'the life of Jesus' (4:10–11) in both weakness and grace.

PART III

Then and now

2 Corinthians and the New Testament

Does 2 Corinthians make a distinctive contribution to the theology of the New Testament? This question would not be asked of the Epistle to the Hebrews. It is unique and its contents are unparalleled in the New Testament. However, 2 Corinthians represents only part of Paul's correspondence with Corinth, which itself is but a portion of his writing output. It is, therefore, not the only exposition of Paul's thought, and it is entirely possible that it merely reiterates what he has said elsewhere.

While possible, this is not very likely. First, letters for Paul were a poor substitute for oral communication;[87] he preferred to deal with problems in person, and in crisis situations he did not hesitate to modify his plans in order to make an urgent visit to a community in trouble, e.g. the intermediate visit to Corinth in the summer of AD 54. He wrote a letter only when he was inescapably committed elsewhere and the matter was of extreme urgency. Second, given the means of letter writing in the first century, the composition of a long letter represented a significant investment of time and energy.[88] It is improbable, therefore, that Paul never merely repeated himself in a letter. He wrote because he had something new to say, something which he hoped would meet the needs of the community in question more adequately. Thus, while the various letters overlap to a certain extent because Paul's basic theology

[87] See S. K. Stowers, *Letter Writing in Greco-Roman Antiquity* (Philadelphia, 1986), 39.
[88] G. Bahr, 'Paul and Letter Writing in the First Century', *CBQ* 28 (1966), 465–77.

remained the same, each epistle contains developments and nuances which do not appear in the others.

2 Corinthians is exceptional in the amount of new material it contains. Paul's reaction in 1 Corinthians to developments at Corinth had succeeded only in alienating an influential block of believers (the Spirit-people). As we have seen, in order to win them back and to wean them from the Judaizers he had to reassess his presentation of the gospel. This meant that he was also forced to rethink his understanding of his ministry because the two were intimately related. This process was tightly focused by the need to counter the vision of ministry being propagated by his opponents, who believed that the authority of the Spirit could only be expressed in power and never in weakness.

Thus the specific contribution of 2 Corinthians to the New Testament lies in three areas: (1) ministry, (2) suffering, and (3) the criteria by which one recognizes the activity of the Spirit. To draw any clear distinction between them, however, would be highly artificial, because, for Paul, the key to each is to be found in the person of Jesus Christ. This was not due simply to the fundamentally Christocentric character of the apostle's thought. In opposition to the Spirit-people, whose attitude said in effect 'Jesus be cursed' (1 Cor. 12:3), Paul had to insist on the importance of the historical Jesus. It was in reflecting on the conditions of the latter's ministry that Paul saw its relevance to his own situation. In the process, he gave new speculative depth to the understanding of Christ's ministry reflected in the gospel tradition. Here we can only sketch the broad outlines, particularly as they appear in 2 Corinthians.

THE MINISTRY OF JESUS AND OTHER CHRISTS

The manner of Christ's ministry was determined by God: 'For our sake he made him to be sin who knew no sin' (2 Cor. 5:21). God willed Christ to be subject to the consequences of sin (cf. pp. 61–2). Jesus was so fully integrated into humanity-needing-salvation that he endured the penalties inherent in its fallen state. Jesus did not save humanity from without. He was not the type of glorious saviour the Spirit-people desired. He saved humanity from within by adopting its condition and transforming it. He became as other human beings in order to reveal to them what they had the potential to become. Thus he suffered as others suffer, and died as others die, even though he in no way merited such affliction.

If this text highlights the divine plan, others emphasize the freedom of Christ's co-operation: 'You know the grace of our Lord Jesus Christ, who, though rich, became poor for your sake' (2 Cor. 8:9). The contrast is between Christ's life as it might have been and his life as it actually was. As sinless, he enjoyed the friendship of God, yet the life he lived exhibited none of the signs of divine favour. It was characterized by material poverty (Matt. 8:20), and culminated in a criminal's death by crucifixion, the most degrading and radical form of impoverishment. The instinct of self-preservation is very deeply rooted. Yet Christ let go of everything, not under duress but by choice. Why?

In order to answer this question Paul takes as his starting point the credal affirmation that 'one died for all' (2 Cor. 5:14; cf. 1 Cor. 15:3). 'For all' expresses the purpose of Christ's life, as does 'for our/your sake' in the two texts just discussed. His suffering and death was a deliberate sacrifice of self in order that others might benefit. The lesson that all must learn from the self-oblation of Christ is that we should live for one another (2 Cor. 5:15). Egocentricity, which for Paul is the essence of enslavement to Sin, must give way to altruism. The fact that Christ chose to die for others underlines in the most graphic way possible the other-directed nature of his being and mission. Prior to Christ, it was taken for granted that the primary goals of one's efforts should be survival, comfort and success. In the light of Christ's radical altruism, such a lifestyle can only be perceived as the 'death' of selfishness. It is the antithesis of genuine 'life' which is totally concerned with benefiting the other.

The essence of authenticity is empowerment, the ability to reach out and enable others. It is this creativity which makes

Christ 'the image of God' (2 Cor. 4:4). In the chapter of
Genesis in which this formula appears (Gen. 1:26–7) God is
presented exclusively as the Creator, and this aspect must
remain the primary referent. As the power of God for salvation
(1 Cor. 1:24) Christ is, like Adam before the fall, 'the image
and glory of God' (1 Cor. 11:7) in the sense that he gives glory
to God by being precisely what the Creator intended.

The effect of this brief outline is to highlight the uniqueness
of Paul's Christology. The creative power which made Christ
the New Adam was exercised in and through poverty and
ignominy. His whole existence was a 'dying' (2 Cor. 4:10), yet
he brought into being 'a new creation' (2 Cor. 5:17). It was
easy for Paul to see this as the archetype of his own situation.
He was conscious of his 'weakness', yet he disposed of a 'power'
(2 Cor. 4:7) which created new communities (2 Cor. 3:2–3).
The power they both channelled, however, belonged to God
(1 Cor. 1:24; 2 Cor. 4:7). It would appear in consequence that
the basis of Paul's identification with Christ, which is the
distinctive feature of his understanding of ministry in
2 Corinthians, was rooted in their shared experience of suffering and pain. Certainly, this is the first aspect of the
relationship which Paul evokes in 2 Corinthians.

He perceives himself as one of the captives destined for
execution at the climax of a Roman victory parade (2 Cor.
2:14). It was not a role which he had chosen. Suffering was a
facet of his ministry over which he had no control (2 Cor.
11:23–8). Since it happened, however, it must be part of God's
plan, and it was up to Paul to discern its meaning, both in
order to make sense of his own life, and in order to reply to the
charges of his opponents.

His first insight is to see such suffering as a prolongation of
the sacrifice of Christ. He is 'the aroma of Christ' (2 Cor. 2:15).
As smoke wafting across the city from the altar conveyed the
fact of a sacrifice to those who were not present in the temple,
so Paul in his wanderings brings the knowledge of Jesus to a
world wider than the little country in which the latter had
lived.

A minister, however, cannot merely preach the passion of

Christ; he must live it. Paul certainly did: 2 Corinthians mentions his sufferings more frequently and more explicitly than any other letter (1:4–10; 4:7–12; 4:16–17; 6:4–10; 7:5; 10:10; 11:23–9; 12:7–10). Natural catastrophes and enemies of all sorts mean that he is continuously in peril of his life: 'while we are alive we are always being given up to death for Jesus' sake' (2 Cor. 4:11). Death shadows his every step; it can strike at any moment. As headed towards a death which seems inevitable, his ministry is a 'dying' which he identifies with that of Jesus, 'always carrying in the body the dying of Jesus' (2 Cor. 4:10). While Paul no more makes a real distinction between the historical Jesus and the risen Christ than the evangelists did, his use of 'Jesus' alone in contexts such as this indicates that he is thinking not of the risen Christ who cannot die, but of the historical Jesus who lived in anticipation of death (e.g. Mark 8:31) and who suffered on the cross. In much more than the physical sense his whole life was a process of 'dying'. The identity of situation and experience inevitably drew Paul to see his ministry as a re-presentation of that of Jesus.[89] He is what Jesus was, a suffering servant.

Once this is grasped, it is not surprising to find Paul applying to his own ministry the Servant Songs of Deutero-Isaiah which, if they did not form the self-understanding of Jesus, were quickly seen to be prophetic of his mission. The formal citation of Isaiah 49:8 in 2 Corinthians 6:2 is complemented by the parallel between Paul's call (Gal. 1;15) and that of the Servant (Isa. 49:1) and by the apostle's use of Isaiah 52:15 to fix the parameters of his mission (Rom. 15:21).[90] If Paul views his own ministry in terms of the prophecies fulfilled

---

89 E. Käsemann's fundamental insight that Paul, through his sufferings, is 'die irdische Manifestation des Christus selbst' ('Die Legitimität des Apostles. Eine Untersuchung zu II Korinther 10–13', *ZNW* 41 (1942), 53) is pushed to absurd lengths by E. Güttgemanns who writes, 'das Subjekt dieses Geschehens ist nicht der Pneumatiker [= Apostel], sondern der Erlöser, der seine Identität mit dem irdischen Jesus, d.h. mit sich selbst demonstriert' (*Der leidende Apostel und sein Herr. Studien zur paulinischen Christologie* (FRLANT 90; Gottingen, 1966), 119). Their interpretation is the consequence of a rigid literalism, which fails to recognize the pervasiveness of analogy in ordinary speech and writing. See also note 94.

90 For more detail see L. Cerfaux, 'Saint Paul et le "Serviteur de Dieu" d'Isaïe', *Studia Anselmiana* 27–8 (1951), 361–65.

by the ministry of Jesus, it can only be because he considers Christ to be active in and through him. Though separated in time, their ministries are unified by a common goal, the salvation of humanity, which is achieved by their communication of the same divine grace.

Moreover, the Apostle's comportment maintains the visibility of authentic humanity, which was the 'life' of Jesus. The 'life of Jesus' is manifested in his body, his mortal flesh (2 Cor. 4:10–11). Paul does not put himself on the same level as Jesus, because what he does would not have been possible without Jesus. None the less, he recognizes that, were Jesus to have been the only one to demonstrate the type of humanity desired by the Creator, its revelation would have been dismissed as irrelevant, a unique case without meaning for the rest of the human race. Paul is deeply conscious of the need of human beings to *see* authentic humanity. They need to be convinced that it is a tangible reality and not merely a utopian ideal, and only a *lived presence* can do this. Thus the ministry of Jesus cannot be prolonged verbally, by preaching alone. Paul has to assume the responsibility of *being Jesus* for his converts.[91]

The explicitness of this presentation of the minister as an *alter Christus* is without parallel in the New Testament.[92] The closest analogies are to be found in Matthew and Luke. The former has the disciples saying (Matt. 10:7) and doing (Matt. 10:8) exactly what Jesus said (Matt. 4:17) and did (Matt. 8–9). The effect of this identification, however, is somewhat diluted by the attribution of the same message to John the Baptist (Matt. 3:2), and by the distinction implicit in the promise of Jesus that he would be with them all days (Matt. 28:20). In Luke equally an identification between Jesus and Paul is only

---

[91] Once this is recognized it becomes clear that Paul's comparison of himself with Moses (2 Cor. 3:7–18) is nothing but a peripheral polemical point. There is no justification for the claim by F. Young and D. F. Ford that 'Moses is the figure on which Paul's ministry is modelled . . . clearly Moses is the "type" or "model" of Paul's role' (*Meaning and Truth in 2 Corinthians* (London, 1987), 82).

[92] My use of the singular 'minister' is purely stylistic, and it is not intended to limit the reference to Paul or to ordained ministers in a church hierarchy. 2 Corinthians makes it clear that *all believers* 'are being changed into his likeness', and so manifest in their bodies the life of Jesus. Note also what is said later in this chapter regarding 2 Corinthians 8–9.

suggested by means of the middle term, 'light of the nations' (Isa. 49:6), which is predicated first of Paul (Acts 13:47) and then of Christ (Acts 26:23).

SUFFERING AND GRACE

The 'life of Jesus' is the most fundamental form of ministry because it demonstrates the *present reality* of grace by highlighting its effect in the personality of the minister. Paul focuses attention on this aspect by the paradoxical statement 'when I am weak then I am strong (2 Cor. 12:10), which is at the heart of his case against his detractors. His intention is to emphasize the discrepancy between what he is socially and what he achieves, with a view to underlining the fact that the visibility of grace, which is the essence of ministry, is conditioned by the situation of the recipient of God's favour (2 Cor. 4:7). Generosity and effectiveness on the part of those who are secure, honoured and wealthy is easily discounted. To give does not put them at risk. They are not diminished by the expenditure of energy. It would be different were they to give *all*, their riches in gift, their persons in service. That would be a gesture which could be explained adequately only in terms of grace.

Only against this background does it become intelligible why Paul *boasts* of his 'weakness' (2 Cor. 12:5–9). He accentuates the precise aspect of his ministry which his opponents would expect him to attempt to hide or explain away. Paradoxically, he makes it his strongest argument, which is validated by the parallel with the ministry of Jesus.

Like all authentic ministers, in worldly terms Paul is powerless, devoid of any social leverage which would make his mission feasible. In human terms his success in founding and nurturing communities is inexplicable. This had always been true, but it is only in 2 Corinthians that he sees it as a dramatic demonstration that 'the transcendent power belongs to God and not to us' (2 Cor. 4:7). The force which draws converts and builds communities can only be 'the grace of God', which is 'the power of Christ' (2 Cor. 12:9–10). It is through Paul that Christ is *seen* to be still active in the world. Christ's power, however, is visible only in its effect (the growth of the church); its contemporary channel (in this case Paul) remains marked by the weakness of the cross; 'He was crucified in weakness . . . we are weak in him' (2 Cor. 13:4). 'Power is made perfect in weakness' (2 Cor. 12:9) in the sense that it is revealed for what it is by the circumstances in which it is deployed – just as the creative love of God becomes visible and effective when Christians in fact love one another (1 John 4:12).

In 1 Corinthians Paul had insisted that love is the being of a Christian: 'without love I am nothing' (13:2).[93] Not surprisingly, therefore, he also sees it as the indispensable ingredient in the minister's manifestation of the 'life of Jesus'. His own lifestyle is characterized by 'love without hypocrisy' (2 Cor. 6:6).[94] It is the antithesis of a calculated affection which strives to please in order to win a response from others. The best illustration of Paul's meaning is his conduct with regard to the church at Corinth. His 'overflowing love' (2 Cor. 2:4) took the form of a harsh letter pointing out their deficiencies, a letter written 'with much affliction of heart and with many tears' (2 Cor. 4:4) both because he knew the pain it would cause and because it put his relationship with the community at risk. He could not be sure that it would have the hoped-for effect, and he waited with deep anxiety for the reaction of the Corinthians (2 Cor. 2:13). Obviously, he acted in this way only because he felt that he had no choice. Paul sought nothing for himself (2 Cor. 7:12). His sole concern was that the Corinthians should perceive what authentic Christianity demanded of them, and the courage and power of his love in fact produced the desired change (2 Cor. 7:9–11). It is in this perspective that the other expressions of his love (2 Cor. 6:11; 7:1; 8:7) must be read. Ministerial love is not sentimental affection, but an active concern which both challenges and enables.

Once again it is distinctive of 2 Corinthians within the New

---

[93] See especially C. Spicq, *Agapé dans le Nouveau Testament. Analyse des textes*, vol. II (Paris, 1959), 71, note 2.

[94] The same authentic love is expected of all believers (2 Cor. 8:8; Rom. 12:9), underlining once again that what Paul says of himself is applicable to every Christian. Cf. Spicq, *Agape*, vol. II, 136–57.

Testament that such love is viewed Christologically.[95] The motive which commands Paul's comportment, the inspiration which ensures his perseverance is the love shown by Christ: 'The love of Christ constrains us' (2 Cor. 5:14). The quality of this love is revealed by the fact that Jesus gave his life for others (2 Cor. 5:15), which Paul – as every Christian must – understands in a directly personal sense: 'he loved *me* and gave himself for *me*' (Gal. 2:20). This conviction leaves him no option but to model his life on the generosity of Christ, and to dedicate himself to bringing others within the orbit of that saving love.

The circumstances of 2 Corinthians forced Paul to focus attention on himself, but we have already seen indications that the portrait of the minister, which he develops, is not unique to him personally. The most fundamental form of the apostolate is existential, which means that it is nothing but the Christian life looked at from another angle.[96] They are two sides of the same coin. Thus, if we abstract from the authority accruing to Paul as the founder of churches, what he says of himself is true of all sincere believers. This aspect appears very clearly in 2 Corinthians 8–9, where what is said of ordinary believers closely parallels what Paul says of himself. In these chapters Paul deals with the ministry of the church as typified by one particular activity, financial assistance to the poor of Jerusalem. The community is apostolic when it affirms its adherence to the gospel (9:13), not merely by words, but by a comportment exhibiting the spontaneous generosity which makes love genuine (8:8, 24). The model of such generosity is Christ, 'who though rich for your sake became poor, so that by his poverty you might become rich' (8:9). That the community represents Christ is not explicit in this context, but it has been evoked previously in the reference to the transformation of

---

95 In relation to its length, no New Testament document speaks of love as frequently as 1 John. Yet in this letter the love of Christ is never once mentioned; it is always the love of the Father.

96 Güttgemanns' attempt to argue that Paul suffered precisely as an apostle and not as a Christian (*Der leidende Apostel*, 27–9) is refuted by what Paul says of the apostolic impact of a suffering community (1 Thess. 1:6–8), and by his claim to belong to a vast fellowship of the sufferings of Christ (Phil. 3:10).

believers into his image (2 Cor. 3:18). Moreover, we cannot forget that in his previous letter to Corinth Paul had insisted that the church is the Body of Christ (1 Cor. 6:15; 12:4–31), i.e. that it is the physical presence of Christ in the world.[97] The highlighting of love in 2 Corinthians as the essential element in this functional identification gives new depth and vigour to the theme of corporate witness, which appears in very schematic form elsewhere in Paul (1 Thess. 1:6–8; Phil. 2:14–16), in the Pastorals,[98] and in the Sermon on the Mount (Matt. 5:16).

The insistence with which Paul emphasizes his existential identity with Jesus reveals the hidden dimension of his claim to be an 'ambassador of Christ' (2 Cor. 5:20). In that context he is primarily concerned with the verbal dimension of his ministry, but by literally re-presenting Christ to the world he also speaks on a much more profound level. The divine message which was Christ is now spoken in and through Paul: 'God is making his appeal through us' (2 Cor. 5:20). He has been 'christed' by God (2 Cor. 1:21) and endowed with the Spirit whose ministry of righteousness he serves (2 Cor. 3:8–9).

RECOGNIZING THE HOLY SPIRIT

From this perspective it becomes clear that Paul's objection to ministers who relied on education and rhetorical ability has a much more solid foundation than at first appears. One could get the impression that he rejected them simply because they were intruders who had invaded his territory and challenged his authority. On the practical level, he recognized that naturally gifted ministers tend to draw converts to *themselves*. What their converts perceive is human wisdom, not the power of God (1 Cor. 2:5). The almost inevitable result is a personality cult and fractionalization of the church. Thus Apollos, almost certainly against his will (1 Cor. 16:12), found himself the centre of a faction within the Corinthian church (1 Cor. 1:12). The situation was exacerbated by the intruders who,

---

[97] This aspect is further developed in my *Becoming Human Together*, 174–98.
[98] See C. Spicq, 'Vie chrétienne et Beauté', in his *Saint Paul. Epîtres Pastorales* (EB; 2nd edn; Paris, 1969), 676–84.

realizing the tastes of the Spirit-people, emphasized their visions and revelations (12:1), their mystical experiences (12:2) and their signs, wonders and mighty works (12:12). These, they claimed, were the guarantee that the Spirit of God was on their side. The ordinariness of Paul, on the contrary, proved his lack of spiritual endowment. This was a much more serious threat to Paul's authority because it was so difficult to counter. Such manifestations appeared to be self-authenticating. Their extraordinary character made questions superfluous. Moreover, they fitted into a pattern of religious experience well-attested in the Greco-Roman world.[99]

Thus Paul could not simply deny the existence of charismatic experiences; neither could he dismiss them as phenomena of the world associated with the worship of false gods. He had accepted them as authentic manifestations of the Spirit in a previous letter (1 Cor. 12–14). Even there, however, he had recognized the necessity for a test which would guarantee the *Christian* character of such experiences. The one he proposed was a public confession; 'no one can say "Jesus is Lord" except by the Holy Spirit' (1 Cor. 12:3).[100] This formulation permits two possible emphases, on 'Jesus' or on 'Lord'. The context suggests that Paul intended the first, because by their negative attitude towards the historical Jesus who suffered and died the Spirit-people were effectively saying 'Jesus be cursed'. These latter, however, would tend to emphasize 'Lord' (cf. 1 Cor. 2:8), and the intruders would certainly have no difficulty in proclaiming the Lordship of Jesus. Thus in 2 Corinthians Paul had to go more deeply into the problem, because believers who professed 'Jesus is Lord' were claiming charismatic experiences which he could not recognize as authentic. The question he had to answer was: what is the specific feature which distinguishes a genuinely Christian charismatic experience from all others?

---

99 A convenient summary of the evidence is provided by J. Dunn, (*Jesus and the Spirit. A Study of the Religious and Charismatic Experience of Jesus and the First Christians as Reflected in the New Testament* (Philadelphia, 1975), 302–7).

100 A similar but not identical test is proposed in 1 John 4:1–3.

Dunn has taken up this question in chapter 10 of his *Jesus and the Spirit*, and the answer he proposes is:

The character of the Christ event is the hallmark of the Spirit. Whatever religious experience fails to reproduce this character in the individual or community, it is thereby self-condemned as delusory or demonic; it is not the work of the eschatological spirit. For the eschatological Spirit is no more and no less than the Spirit of Christ. (pp. 321–2)

This is made more specific a little later: 'As soon as charismatic experience becomes an experience only of the exalted Christ and not also of the crucified Jesus, it loses its distinctively Christian character' (p. 331). In order to justify this reply Dunn draws on all the Pauline letters without concern for their chronological order or specific concerns. This approach can be justified only if Paul gives a similar answer in the one epistle in which he had to provide a criterion for authentic ecstatic experience, namely 2 Corinthians. Otherwise there is danger of creating a synthesis which Paul never entertained.

In a number of passages of 2 Corinthians Jesus Christ and Holy Spirit are intimately associated. The first is in the double set of paired participles in 1:21–2: 'The one establishing us with you in Christ and having 'christed' us in God, who is the one having sealed us and having given the earnest of the Spirit in our hearts.' Much could be said about these verses,[101] but here it is sufficient to highlight the central thrust. The effect of the presence of the Spirit is to assimilate believers to Jesus. In context, the allusion is to the consistent fidelity of Jesus (1:19), but the underlying principle is more generic, as the second passage shows. The essential point of 3:18 is that God acts through the Spirit to transform believers into the image of Jesus. Jesus, of course, is now the exalted Christ, but when Paul evokes this latter aspect in 2 Corinthians he is careful to balance it by a reference to the crucifixion (13:4), which is consistently emphasized throughout the letter (1:5; 2:15; 4:10; 5:14–15; 8:9). In practice, therefore, the presence of the Spirit is attested by a comportment specified by the 'dying of Jesus'

---

[101] See in particular I. de la Potterie, 'L'Onction du chrétien par la foi', *Biblica* 40 (1959), 12–69; and V. P. Furnish, *II Corinthians* (AB; Garden City, NY, 1984), 147–50.

(4:10). Finally, believers are given the Spirit (1:22; 5:5), but it is in them in the form of Jesus Christ (13:5). For 2 Corinthians, therefore, only an existence marked by the cross ('weakness'; 13:4a) and inspired by its motive ('love'; 5:14) manifests the activity of the Spirit. This means that Dunn's thesis is rooted historically, and he highlights its eschatological relevance thus: 'Where they (Paul's opponents at Corinth) thought of the Spirit as a power of the *already* which swallows up the *not yet* in forceful speech and action, Paul thought of it as a power which reinforces the *not yet*.'[102] Paul's subsequent thought on the Holy Spirit was governed by the insight of 2 Corinthians which he condensed into lapidary phrases with the exegetical genitive, 'the Spirit of Jesus Christ' (Phil. 1:19), 'the Spirit of God's Son' (Gal. 4:6), and 'the Spirit of Christ' (Rom. 8:9). Apart from the highly ambiguous mention of 'the Spirit of Jesus' in Acts 16:7, the relationship between Jesus and the Spirit is developed only in the Fourth Gospel where, however, the perspective is slightly different, because John's concern is not identical with that of Paul.[103]

The three facets of ministry summarized above represent the distinctive contribution of 2 Corinthians to the New Testament. In Paul's mind, however, they were but a part of his total understanding of ministry, whose theological framework appears in his very first letter:

> We know, brethren, that God has chosen you, because our gospel came to you, not in word alone, but in power and in the Holy Spirit and in all abundance, as you know what sort of persons we were among you and for you, and you became imitators of us and of the Lord, receiving the word in much affliction with joy inspired by the Holy Spirit. (1 Thess. 1:4–6)

Elements of this extremely suggestive outline are filled out in other letters as Paul develops his theology in dialogue with his communities. The practical realities of church life also had an impact: who enjoyed authority in the community and how was it to be exercised? Were ministers simply to emerge or should

---

102 *Jesus and the Spirit*, 330; my emphases.
103 See Dunn, *Jesus and the Spirit*, 350–3.

they be appointed? Were women eligible for ministerial roles?
These and other questions would have to be answered in any
complete exposition of Paul's theology of ministry. To do so
here, however, would take us too far afield, particularly if his
liberating vision were to be contrasted with the bureaucratic
concept of ministry reflected in the pastoral Epistles.
Moreover, it would cut across other contributions to this series.
Hence it must suffice here to underline that the profound
Christological dimension of ministry introduced by 2 Corinthians is undoubtedly one of the summits of Paul's theological achievement.[104]

[104] From an immense bibliography on ministry in the New Testament the following
are of particular utility. H. von Campenhausen, *Kirchliches Amt und geistliche
Vollmacht in den ersten drei Jahrhunderten* (BHT 14; Tübingen, 1953). E. Käsemann,
'Ministry and Community in the New Testament', in his *Essays on New Testament
Themes* (SBT; London, 1964). *Le Ministère et les ministères selon le Nouveau Testament.
Dossier exégétique et réflection théologique*, ed. J. Delorme (Paris, 1973).

CHAPTER 12

The significance of 2 Corinthians for today

2 Corinthians is a document which can be read with profit by any Christian of any period of history. Although occasioned by the situation of a particular first-century church, the passion of Paul's response still has the power to stir the hearts of those who perceive the gallantry of unaided struggle against misunderstanding and betrayal. It is an intensely personal letter, but the profundity of Paul's insights ensures that it speaks to all generations. Its fundamental theme is the paradox of human existence as touched by God.[105] The ramifications are virtually limitless. If I here select a number of examples to show the relevance of 2 Corinthians, it is not that they are necessarily the most important. They simply appear particularly apposite to a world approaching the end of the twentieth century, and illustrate how we might permit the letter to challenge us.

THE MEANING OF SUFFERING

No one can compute the measure of human suffering, but in this century wars have never been more numerous or more destructive; famine has seldom been more frequent or more widespread; diseases caused by humanity's contamination of its environment are on the increase. The problem of such suffering has always preoccupied those who believe in creation

---

105 According to F. Young and D. F. Ford the basic thrust of 2 Corinthians is summed up in the formula 'the glory of God', which, among other aspects, 'is the dynamic of transformation in Christian life and it is intrinsically social, to be participated in through a community of those who reflect it together' (*Meaning and Truth in 2 Corinthians* (London, 1987), 259).

and providence, and Paul could not avoid concerning himself with it.

With one minor exception – the *ad hominem* argument in 1 Corinthians 11:30 – he does not justify suffering as merited divine punishment inflicted on sinners, which is a significant departure from Old Testament precedents. Even though he uses sacrificial language of his own sufferings and those of others,[106] there is not the slightest hint that he saw suffering as a sacrifice designed to propitiate an angry God.

It has been argued that Paul saw human suffering as the inevitable consequence of the life of the Spirit having to express itself through the body of death.[107] There is some justification for this view, and at least it would explain why Paul considered suffering to be inevitable. Like Jesus, he took it for granted that he and his converts would experience pain. Others, however, had come to the same conclusion on very different grounds.[108] Paul did not need suffering to remind him that he was living the eschatological tension of the *not yet*. It sufficed to know that Jesus had been raised from the dead and that the general resurrection was yet to come (1 Cor. 15).

For Paul the pastor, if suffering was inevitable, there was little to be gained by knowing the reason why. If it was a given of human existence, the only serious question for a Christian was how it could be integrated into the divine plan of salvation. Because of his vocation, Paul tended to see everything in missionary terms. Inevitably, therefore, he was led to see suffering less as a problem than as an opportunity. Thus the question which he asked himself concerning the sufferings of Christ, his own and those of his converts was: how do such sufferings serve the furtherance of God's plan for humanity?

---

[106] See especially A.-M. Denis, 'La Fonction apostolique et la liturgie nouvelle en Esprit. Etude thématique des métaphores pauliniennes du culte nouveau', *Revue des Sciences Philosophiques et Theologiques* 42 (1958), 401–36, 617–56.

[107] J. Dunn, *Jesus and the Spirit. A Study of the Religious and Charismatic Experience of Jesus and the First Christians as Reflected in the New Testament* (Philadelphia, 1975), 327.

[108] Homer commented 'The fates have given humanity a patient soul' (*Iliad*, bk 24, 1:49), because 'Thus have the gods spun the thread for wretched mortals: that they live in grief while they themselves are without cares' (*Iliad*, bk 24, 1:525). The same pessimistic attitude towards reality is reflected in Virgil's remark, 'Better days, perhaps, await the wretched' (*Aeneid*, bk 12, 1:153).

The meaning he sought was not speculative but practical. The 'why' of suffering might be of interest to those who had time to indulge themselves in such reflection. He, however, had a mission to accomplish, and his instinct was to integrate suffering into that quest.

If the God who caused or permitted his sufferings had also confided to him the responsibility of spreading the faith, Paul reasoned, the two had to be related. The same was true of Jesus, whose suffering and death Paul could only interpret as the most profound clue to the meaning of the mission of Christ.[109] In the case of the latter it revealed creative love to be the essential ingredient of authentic humanity. This convinced Paul that his own sufferings could have the same revelatory value, and so his 'weakness' became the contemporary means whereby the power of God in Christ was manifested. The discrepancy between what he *was* and what he *achieved* was thrust on the attention of the world by his sufferings. This discrepancy made him transparent. His success pointed beyond his personality to God. Grace became visible in history.

The value of this insight for a world in which there is so much unavoidable suffering needs no emphasis. The fact of famine, for example, or civil war has led many to renounce God or to treat him as irrelevant. The Good News is mocked by the senselessness of a mud-slide which destroys a village. Can God still be involved with his creation, if such tragedies happen with sickening regularity? The solution of some, a Sartre or a Camus, is to proclaim the absurdity of existence. Such defeatism has been, and always will be, unpalatable to the majority, who will struggle to find meaning in life. It is these who want to believe. But to do so they need a *contemporary* demonstration of divine power. It is not enough for them to know that grace was once active in history. They want to be sure that it is active *now*. For Paul it is this need which gives meaning to the lives of those who suffer. As followers of Christ they should not focus primarily on their own need for relief. They should seize the opportunity to articulate the gospel in the only way a weary

109 See my *Becoming Human Together*, 33–57.

and cynical world will accept. In their bearing and achievements they can *manifest* the power of grace in action here and
now.

AID TO THE POOR

What has just been said might give the impression that Paul
placed such a value on suffering as a means of propagating the
gospel that it should not be alleviated. Nothing could be
further from the truth. In 2 Corinthians 8–9 Paul deals at
length with the collection designed to alleviate the misery of
the poor of Jerusalem. This collection is immediately evocative
of current national and international efforts to put together the
vast sums of money necessary to provide food for the victims of
famine or to furnish aid to those whose lives have been
irrevocably changed by natural disasters. Paul would applaud
such efforts wholeheartedly, because suffering is not a good
thing in itself. Where possible, it should be given relief. Only
when it is inescapable should one try to find a positive aspect.

The suffering of the poor in Jerusalem was not unavoidable.
The Christians in the diaspora could do something about it,
and Paul was very anxious that they should. In his attempts to
motivate the Corinthians to part with their cash he is reminiscent of modern fund-raisers. His goal, however, was much
more complex than the sums on which fund-raisers set their
sights. The extra dimensions of which he insists are supremely
relevant to participation in contemporary relief efforts.

Firstly Paul emphasizes the obligations of wealth. In his eyes
material prosperity is the result of grace (2 Cor. 9:8; cf. 1 Tim.
6:17). God's gifts, however, are never without a purpose; 'you
are enriched in every way *for all forms of generosity*' (2 Cor. 9:11).
Surplus wealth in one part of our world is part of God's plan for
dealing with misery and pain in another part. Although he
could, God will not act directly in history, because he has
chosen human intermediaries (1 Cor. 3:5–9). He has made
himself dependent on human co-operation. Within the framework of responsibility created by his gifts, it is we who are
accountable for the perception and solution of the problems of

poverty and disease. To give is not a matter of choice but of obligation. We are the hands and ears of God, and if we do not listen to the cry of the poor, effectively God does not hear.

Secondly, for Paul generosity is integral to the very being of the Christians. It is a gesture which enables the recipients to achieve a new life, and such creative empowerment is what makes believers the 'image of God'. They become fully human in virtue of a generosity of the standard established by the complete self-giving of Jesus (2 Cor. 8:9). Thus the attitude of the giver is more important than the value of the contribution (2 Cor. 8:12). It must be given freely as an expression of love; it should not be tinged with reluctance or be the consequence of external pressure (2 Cor. 9:7). Cold charity is an insult to the recipient, but true generosity is 'a gracious work' (2 Cor. 8:7). The gesture becomes a channel of grace in so far as it implies the gift of self, which becomes an existential proclamation of the good news. Grace is concretized and manifested in generosity inspired by love. To give out of a sense of guilt or shame, as is the case in so many contemporary situations when graphic pictures make the pain of the contrast between viewer and victim unendurable, is not good enough. 2 Corinthians shows why it diminishes both donor and recipient. It is also a missed opportunity to demonstrate the love of God in action. Paul incites us to think in missionary terms.

FORMS OF MINISTRY

His letters indicate that Paul thought of himself as responsible for a number of communities. The closest parallel to this situation among twentieth-century ecclesiastical communions are those in which a single individual, a bishop or equivalent, has charge of a number of local communities, i.e. parishes, which constitute a diocese. In theory, the structural model is the same as that of the Pauline churches, but in practice there is a huge difference, which 2 Corinthians challenges us to face.

The model which dominates in today's episcopal churches is that of the Pastoral Letters,[110] which reflect, not the authentic

---

[110] See Spicq, *Pastorales*, 65–84.

Pauline model, but its corruption through adaptation to the expectations of society. Bishops appoint ministers in the local communities, generally without any consultation. Their role is that of administrators who appoint lesser functionaries. In many churches these have to be male, and in the Roman Catholic tradition also celibate. In consequence, the autonomy of the local church is severely diminished. Initiative and originality at the local level is stifled. The voice of the Spirit is silenced.

It would be unreasonable to advocate a return to the purely charismatic model of church authority, which some scholars have claimed to find in the Corinthian correspondence.[111] A community without structures is nonsense, and it was not the Pauline ideal. The anarchy inherent in total freedom, can only be intensified by the unpredictability of spiritual gifts, and unless the community acquires stability through traditionalization or rationalization it will inevitably disintegrate. Thus, in order to survive, a community needs some degree of institutionalization. The real question, therefore, in the perspective of a critique of today's churches is: what type and what degree of institutionalization is appropriate to a genuinely Christian community?

2 Corinthians does not address this question, but it does provide the fundamental criterion by which authentic ministers should be assessed and selected. Ministers should manifest in their comportment 'the life of Jesus' (2 Cor. 4:10–11). Their behaviour should be animated by a self-sacrificing love which is the channel of divine grace here and now. Their basic message should be 'Imitate me as I imitate Christ' (1 Cor. 11:1).

2 Corinthians, therefore, invites us to contemplate the consequences of the application of this criterion to all levels of ministry. One can predict that, as a minimum, a form of institutionalization, which has proved stifling and sterile, should gradually give way to a framework in which the Spirit can again speak and act in freedom.

---

[111] For example, E. Käsemann, 'Ministry and Community in the New Testament', in his *Essays on New Testament Themes* (SBT; London, 1964).

The three examples, which I have selected to draw attention to the contemporary relevance of 2 Corinthians, all serve in their own way to highlight the basic reason why this document is of perennial significance. Paul finds the meaning of suffering, the explanation of the incentive to generosity, and the reason for the effectiveness of ministry, in the person of Jesus Christ. Most believers live out of what R. Scroggs has called 'a covert Unitarianism'.[112] A vague theism permits them to use the concept of the will of God to justify a palpably unchristian lifestyle, which even for them has little meaning. The fundamental relevance of 2 Corinthians is that it forces us to restore Christ to the centre of Christianity. To be consistently Christocentric in our thoughts and deeds is a lesson of which all need to be reminded again and again. That was Paul's life, and nowhere is it more evident than in 2 Corinthians.

---

[112] *Christology in Paul and John. The Reality and the Revelation of God* (Proclamation Commentaries; Philadelphia, 1988), 3.

Further reading

BACKGROUND

Meeks, W. A., *The First Urban Christians. The Social World of the Apostle Paul*, New Haven and London, 1983. (To date, the most thorough social analysis of the Christian community at Corinth, although the data has to be separated from material derived from other Pauline churches.)

Murphy-O'Connor, J., *St. Paul's Corinth. Texts and Archaeology*, Wilmington, 1983. (Collects and translates all the Greek and Latin references to Corinth and combines them with the results of archaeological excavations to create a vivid picture of the first-century city.)

Theissen, G., *The Social Setting of Pauline Chritianity. Essays on Corinth*, Philadelphia, 1982. (An illuminating analysis of aspects of the social history of Corinth.)

SCIENTIFIC COMMENTARIES

These are distinguished from those in the next section by the demands they make on the reader in terms of knowledge of Greek and extensive background information. Some, though old, can still be consulted with great profit.

Allo, E.-B., *Saint Paul. Seconde Epître aux Corinthiens* (Etudes Bibliques), Paris, 1937. (Remarkable for its excursus offering exhaustive discussions of eighteen particularly controverted points.)

Betz, H.-D., *2 Corinthians 8 and 9. A Commentary on Two Administrative Letters of the Apostle Paul* (Hermeneia), Philadelphia, 1985. (Although unsuccessful in its attempt to prove that 2 Corinthians 8 and 9 were originally two independent letters, and insufficient in its grasp of Pauline theology, this commentary is important for its treatment of the form of ancient letters and its collection of contemporary parallels.)

Bultmann, R., *Der Zweite Brief an die Korinther* (Meyer Kommentar), Göttingen, 1976; English translation Minneapolis, 1985. (Posthumously published exegetical lecture notes without theological development.)

Furnish, V. P., *II Corinthians* (Anchor Bible), Garden City, NY, 1984. (This comprehensive commentary is designed for experts, but is accessible to non-specialists in its synthetic sections which expound Paul's theology with clarity and profundity.)

Martin, R. P., *2 Corinthians* (World Biblical Commentary), Waco, TX, 1986. (In the tradition of solid evangelical scholarship. Noteworthy for its extensive bibliographies, and for its insightful location of 2 Corinthians in the framework of Paul's life.)

Plummer, A., *A Critical and Exegetical Commentary on the Second Epistle of St Paul to the Corinthians* (International Critical Commentary), Edinburgh, 1915. (The classic English commentary which is still valuable for its philological interpretation.)

Windisch, H., *Der zweite Korintherbrief* (Meyer Kommentar), Gottingen, 1924. (The quality of this great – some would say, the greatest – commentary is underlined by its 1970 reprinting edited by G. Strecker.)

POPULAR COMMENTARIES

These lack scientific apparatus but not scientific quality. The pastoral tone often enshrines highly original insights.

Barrett, C. K., *The Second Epistle to the Corinthians* (Black's NT Commentaries), London, 1973. (Easily the best popular commentary. Written with extraordinary clarity and perception, it discusses all the problems of the letter in such a way as to be intelligible to non-specialists and illuminating to the expert.)

Best, E., *Second Corinthians* (Interpretation), Atlanta, GA, 1987. (An insightful commentary designed to assist teaching and preaching by discerning the meaning of the text for faith and life.)

Carrez, M., *La Deuxième Epître de saint Paul aux Corinthiens* (Commentaire du NT, deuxième série), Geneva, 1986. (Although very obscure in its discussion of the integrity of 2 Corinthians, its penetrating analysis of the text exhibits a constant concern to highlight the pastoral relevance of Paul's thought.)

STUDIES

These deal synthetically with major themes within 2 Corinthians, but often include material from other epistles.

Dunn, J. D. G., *Jesus and the Spirit. A Study of the Religious and Charismatic Experience of Jesus and the First Christians as Reflected in the New Testament*, London, 1975. (Part 3 of this wide-ranging study deals with Paul's understanding of the role of the Holy Spirit in the Pauline communities.)

Collange, J.-F., *Enigmes de la deuxième épître de Paul aux Corinthiens. Etude exégétique de 2 Cor. 2:14–7:4* (SNTS Monograph Series), Cambridge, 1972. (Argues the highly controversial hypothesis that 2:14–7:4 was not only an independent letter, but that it originally existed in two different versions. None the less, it contains many useful observations of detail.)

Holmberg, B., *Paul and Power. The Structure of Authority in the Primitive Church as Reflected in the Pauline Epistles*, Philadelphia, 1980. (A sophisticated analysis in sociological categories of the nature of charismatic authority and the distribution of power in the churches founded by Paul.)

Murphy-O'Connor, J., *Becoming Human Together. The Pastoral Anthropology of St. Paul*, Wilmington, 1983. (An overview of Paul's theology permitting 2 Corinthians to be seen in the framework of his whole thought.)

Plank, K. A., *Paul and the Irony of Affliction* (SBL Semeia Studies), Atlanta, GA, 1987. (An extremely insightful treatment of 'power in weakness' from the perspective of rhetorical criticism, which provides a fresh appreciation of Paul's skill as a writer and of his intuition as a practical psychologist.)

Rissi, M., *Studien zur zweiten Korintherbrief. Der alte Bund – der Prediger – der Tod* (Abhandlungen zur Theologie des Alten und Neuen Testaments), Zurich, 1969. (Sketches the positions of Paul and his opponents on the Old Testament and death. Must be read critically.)

Young, F. and D. F. Ford, *Meaning and Truth in 2 Corinthians* (Biblical Foundations in Theology), London, 1987. (A pioneering effort to combine exegesis and theology, which also invites the reader to become conscious of all that is involved in trying to understand 2 Corinthians.)

Index